PRAISE FOR JASON MERCHEY and
THE **VALUES OF THE WISE SERIES**

"The VALUES OF THE WISE series is a treasury of ideas, thoughts, and feelings that represent the best of humane ideals. I hope it will be widely read because it could be a wonderful influence on the thinking and behavior of us all."

HOWARD ZINN, PH.D., Professor Emeritus of History, Boston University; Author of *The Twentieth Century*

"I love this book! It's a great compilation."

ANITA RODDICK, Founder of The Body Shop; Author of *A Revolution in Kindness*; Progressive social activist

"Jason Merchey has made available a valuable compilation; it is a rich selection of quotations relating to an array of virtues. His is a book I will turn to in my work on character and ethics education, and in searching for wisdom in my daily life."

BERNICE LERNER, PH.D., Center for the Advancement of Ethics & Character, Boston University

"Reading the wise quotations in this book is like taking sips from a snifter of finely-aged brandy."

PETER B. RAABE, PH.D., Philosopher & philosophical counselor; Author of three books on philosophical counseling, including *Philosophical Counseling: Theory and Practice*

"VALUES OF THE WISE is a wonderful collection of wisdom with powerful messages...."

> **DAVID B. WEXLER, PH.D.,** Director, Relationship Training Institute;
> Author of *When Good Men Behave Badly: Change Your Behavior,*
> *Change Your Relationship*

"This is a wonderful book; a tribute to humane values."

> **JACINTA M. AERNAN, M.A.,** Coordinator,
> The Alliance for African Assistance

"As someone who is writing on altruism and compassion, apology and forgiveness – Merchey's book has become very useful and I highly appreciate this valuable compendium of quotations. I look forward to using some of the wise words in parts of my work. I highly recommend this book for anyone who is interested in kindness, compassion, and social responsibility because it throws some light on the need for wisdom and caring."

> **SAMUEL OLINER, PH.D.,** Emeritus Professor of Sociology, Humboldt State
> University; Founder/Director of the Altruistic Personality and Prosocial
> Behavior Institute; Author of numerous publications on the Holocaust,
> altruism, prosocial behavior, and race/ethnic relations, including *Do*
> *Unto Others: Extraordinary Acts of Ordinary People* and *The Altruistic*
> *Personality: Rescuers of Jews in Nazi Europe* (with Pearl Oliner, Ph.D.)

"We all need inspiration and role models; we all grow and learn from each other. The quotations in VALUES OF THE WISE provide just that – inspiration and knowledge for our journey together."

> **DEBORAH LINDHOLM,** Executive Director, Foundation for Women

"Like a medieval monastic scribe illuminating manuscripts for the few, Jason Merchey is compiling the wisdom of the ages for the many – a cornucopia of insightful treasures."

> **MICHAEL TOMS,** Co-founder and host of New Dimensions World
> Broadcasting Network; Author of *A Time for Choices: Deep Dialogues for*
> *Deep Democracy* and Co-author of *True Work: Doing What You Love and*
> *Loving What You Do*

"The Left rarely talks about values anymore, which is a shame given the deep humanistic roots of radical politics. Merchey has written an essential and beautiful book that might jumpstart that conversation. VALUES OF THE WISE ought to be required reading for anyone interested in changing the world, for changing the world begins with changing how we think about how to live our lives."

ROBIN KELLEY, PH.D., Professor of African American Studies & Anthropology, Columbia University; Author of *Freedom Dreams: The Black Radical Imagination*

"VALUES OF THE WISE stands out among compilations of great quotations and remarkable thoughts. It is a collection of positive, uplifting statements from writers, speakers, and observers from all time periods and walks of life. It will inspire you to pursue your noblest goals and dreams. You'll find yourself turning to it again and again."

SCOTT FARRELL, Founder, *Chivalry Today*

"...a fascinating and useful tour of the pearls of human wisdom. No one could read this book without coming away more thoughtful about his or her own life."

MICHAEL E. KERR, M.D., Director, Bowen Center for the Study of the Family, Georgetown University; Author of *Family Evaluation* (with Murray Bowen)

"VALUES OF THE WISE is a great resource for professional philosophers and all seekers of wisdom. The book contains a comprehensive and inspiring selection of quotations from great thinkers and cultural traditions which can be used to stimulate class discussion as well as one's own thought process."

JUDITH A. BOSS, PH.D., Visiting Scholar in Philosophy and the Center for BioMedical Ethics, Brown University; Author of *Analyzing Moral Issues, Ethics for Life,* and *Perspectives in Ethics*

JASON A. MERCHEY

"To aspire to live a life of value – a life grounded in profound wisdom ascribed to great minds over the ages – is ambitious and inspiring. This book is a wonderful resource; a great gift to every 'student of life' regardless of age! I recommend it highly – a must for those seeking wisdom and inspiration."

> RENEE BARNETT TERRY, PH.D., Dean of Student Affairs, Revelle College – University of California, San Diego

"...an outstanding collection of musings on doing something significant with one's time and energy. Its range and insight are impressive."

> CLAYTON DUBE, UCLA Asia Institute

"One of the many illuminating quotations in this provocative compilation is Shakespeare's 'There is no darkness but ignorance.' Like so many of the aphorisms that VALUES OF THE WISE brings to light, this little gem demystifies tragedy by placing its origins in the realm of the knowable. It also typifies the constructive and eye-opening character of Merchey's highly original collection."

> ROBERT W. FULLER, PH.D., Physicist, educator, and social activist; Former President of Oberlin College; Author of *Somebodies & Nobodies: Overcoming the Abuse of Rank*

"VALUES OF THE WISE is an indispensable anthology of apt and anodyne aphorisms."

> LOU MARINOFF, PH.D., Author of *Plato, Not Prozac!* and *The Big Questions: How Philosophy Can Change Your Life*

"The insightful concept of a 'life of value' provides one with a realistic and potent source to facilitate one's growth as well as solve many of humanity's problems."

> ADRIENNE McFADD, PH.D., Licensed psychologist/psychotherapist

"Merchey has done it again – a feast of thoughtful, carefully compiled words of wisdom to nourish us all. VALUES OF THE WISE is an invaluable addition to everyone's reference desk."

> MAX WEISMANN, Co-Founder and Director of The Mortimer J. Adler Center for the Study of the Great Ideas

"VALUES OF THE WISE books are cornerstones for our collective thinking. Culled from history, they perpetuate the wisdom and strength sorely needed in our global community as we seek peace and justice for all."

> JENNI PRISK, Founder of Voices of Women, a grass-roots organization dedicated to peace and justice

"VALUES OF THE WISE books are profound and inspirational. I keep them on my coffee table."

> JONATHAN DOLHENTY, PH.D., Director, The Center for Applied Philosophy

BUILDING
A LIFE OF
VALUE

BUILDING
A LIFE OF
VALUE

TIMELESS WISDOM
TO INSPIRE AND
EMPOWER US

JASON A. MERCHEY

VALUES OF THE WISE SERIES
VOLUME I

LITTLE MOOSE PRESS
Santa Barbara, CA

Building a Life of Value: Timeless Wisdom to Inspire and Empower Us

Copyright © 2005 Jason A. Merchey

First Edition

Library of Congress Cataloging-in-Publication Data
Merchey, Jason A.
   Building a life of value : timeless wisdom to inspire and empower us / Jason A. Merchey.-- 1st ed.
     p. cm. -- (Values of the wise series ; v. 1)
   Includes bibliographical references and index.
   ISBN 0-9720227-6-7 (alk. paper)
       1. Values--Quotations, maxims, etc. 2. Ethics--Quotations, maxims, etc.
       3. Conduct of life--Quotations, maxims, etc. 4. Wisdom--Quotations, maxims, etc.
       I. Title. II. Series: Merchey, Jason A. Values of the wise series ; v. 1.
   BD435.M45 2004
   170'.44--dc22

                                        2004021328

Published by Little Moose Press
510 Castillo, Suite #304
Santa Barbara, CA 93101
www.littlemoosepress.com

Printed and bound in the United States of America

Cover and book design by Patricia Bacall

Cover photographs by Douglas Reid Fogelson

Author photo by Jan Phillips

Illustrations by Thomas Gaebel

DEDICATION

I dedicate this book to you, the reader,
that you may be inspired.

CONTENTS

BUILDING A LIFE OF VALUE

ACKNOWLEDGMENTS

Who I am today is inextricably bound to my circle of family, friends, and others. I would like to thank my mother, who primarily raised me and is originally responsible for the trajectory on which I have been for three decades. I offer appreciation to my father, one of the clear voices of wisdom and morality in my life. My grandma Esther played a tremendous role raising and teaching me. I wish to acknowledge Stanley Westreich, without whose benefaction this book might not have come to fruition.

I owe gratitude and respect to the diverse group of thinkers and writers whose words fulfill me so. The countless sources from which I have identified these quotations not only provided me with much meaning over the years, but also made this work possible. Sources include conversations, newspaper reports, songs, poetry, lectures, daydreaming, compilations, and original works.

I wish to thank Janet Clemento and Ellen Reid for their effort, guidance, and creative spirit. Dana Wassarman, Gina Gerboth, Brookes Nohlgren, Patricia Bacall, Ellen W. Stiefler, and Laren Bright assisted in specialized ways to bring this wonderful tome to life. Jan Phillips, Michelle Price, Jenni Prisk, and H. Roy Kim contributed to the development of *Building a Life of Value* with their vision and creativity. John Marshall earns special gratitude for his counsel and assistance tracking down some of the sharpest examples of values humanity has to offer.

You, the reader, have my appreciation, for by purchasing this book you are contributing to keeping these ideas dusted off and getting good use.

*"BE THE CHANGE
YOU WISH TO SEE
IN THE WORLD"*

— GANDHI

VALUES OF THE WISE SERIES
VOLUME I

PREFACE

This book is about living a joyous, fulfilling, and humane life – *"a life of value."* I am pleased to share this compilation of timeless wisdom that brings great thinking to life and illuminates the subject of values from many angles. This optimistic and intriguing collection of quotations reflects what the brilliant Albert Einstein knew: "The ideals that have lighted my way have been kindness, beauty, and truth." These ideals have moved me, shaped me, and continue to challenge me; I hope they inspire you as well.

You use your values every day. The questions are, Which values guide you? How did you come to them? Are you excited and fulfilled by these particular values? This is a momentous time in history, and values are critical to its unfolding. What we believe and value will shape the very future that lay ahead of us. Building a foundation on solid values is an essential part of creating a meaningful and responsible life.

My hope is that you will use this book as an inspirational reference tool to prompt new thoughts about your own values. Any quotation can be used for your own reflection or to spark a dialogue with another person. I have found these to be the most compelling thoughts on record about the *values of the wise* – humanity's highest aspirations. And it may be an interesting challenge to ask yourself or a friend, "How does this quote help to define Truth? or Integrity? or Tolerance?" for example. These 38 values and virtues, incorporated into 14 themed chapters, are meant to stimulate thinking and communication, from living rooms to classrooms to boardrooms.

I look back and marvel at how deeply I have been motivated and intrigued by the pursuit of wisdom. Since my childhood, I've been interested in the values of the wise – the values that have shaped the world. I count myself lucky to live in this time and place, and to be able to dedicate myself to the study of our greatest creations. In fact, when I was in college, I was inducted into the honor society *Phi Beta Kappa*, which in Greek stands for "Love of Wisdom: The Guide of Life."

How did I come to be so intrigued with ideas such as these? I think it is the same awe that has excited humans since we first gazed up at the stars and wondered what they were, or fashioned idols such as the female fertility symbol, or developed the concept of law. I was drawn to humane ideals and humanistic principles in the same way that so many others before me were. It is human nature to be touched deeply by deep ideas. If we are going to survive and thrive in this century, and for centuries to come, it will be our conscious and embodied values that will guide us.

During the time I was navigating through early adolescence, most of my beliefs were challenged. I needed something solid on which to base my self-worth, my understanding of the world, and my aspirations – and I couldn't rely on my peers, my family, my religion, or my nation. Little could assuage my angst during those dark times. But values – those human creations that seem to me like giant, perfect marble statues – lit the way for me. Reading the thoughts and words of great thinkers and fresh voices moved me from angst to enthusiasm, from self-doubt to self-awareness. It rang true when someone said to me once, "It's as though Socrates saved you." Since I found philosophy enlightening but complex, I chose to dedicate myself to studying psychology to gain a greater understanding of myself and to become helpful to others. But it remains philosophy, the ancient love of wisdom, that captures my heart. I find that a fusion of philosophy and psychology sheds the brightest light on values and virtues such as peace and courage.

How did I come to view these particular values as *the ones to which the wise aspire and seek to cultivate within themselves?* I've watched how values play out in individual lives, especially in children. A young child will remark, "That's not fair!" calling for justice. If a boy takes another's toy, he is trying to show strength. A girl giving a flower to her mother is practicing magnanimity. A baby who cries at a distressing scene is longing for peace. The little "ham" who sings without embarrassment embodies lightheartedness.

In the beginning I used reason and experience to establish a worthy set of distilled ideas. A survey of history as well as envisioning what we need to thrive in the future suggested evidence for these particular values standing out as humanity's highest aspirations. There is a breadth and depth to this set that is clear: *love* is not specifically named but it is represented to a large degree by *dedication* and *passion*. *Beauty* is part of *vision, passion,* and *self-awareness*. *Goodness* seems to me to be better described by ideals such as *magnanimity, morality,* and *kindness*.

How did I begin? I recall wondering one night what *honor* really means. It is a lofty and elusive concept. I looked it up in the dictionary and on the Internet, finding only partial and shallow definitions. I thought, "Many of the quotations that I've been collecting since my first semester of college ought to enlighten me on this deep and broad topic." The eminently wise philosophy professor, Denis Hickey, required us to memorize wonderful quotations such as the following by the Lebanese poet Kahlil Gibran: "Keep me away from the wisdom which does not weep, the philosophy which does not laugh, and the greatness which does not bow before children." Greatness bowing before children – what a beautiful thing! This meshed very well with my admiration and love for children, and I felt a sense of excitement imagining such ideas.

How did this work come to fruition? It's a challenge to answer, but I do believe it is my "life's work" as my mother puts it, who has been the most remarkable influence on my path in life. Or, maybe it was the incredible ideas my father introduced me to, such as knowledge, modesty, dedication, humor, and magnanimity. Perhaps it is *Values of the Wise's* Director of Marketing and Development Janet Clemento's belief in me and in the power of a person to grow using will. I appreciate John A. Marshall talking with me about the values and gathering examples he found in stacks of books. And I was always able to find meaning digging in, distilling information down for easier comprehension by you, the readers, to whom I wish to be useful.

All those influences and more account for how and why I spent so much time and energy thinking, reading, training, typing, risking, envisioning, and hoping. I give my heartfelt praise to those incredible men and women who have pursued these values and left thoughts behind

JASON A. MERCHEY

like messages in bottles for centuries. Their thoughts have been a lifeline – saving some lives and helping the rest of us live better ones. I love opening these bottles that have washed upon the shore, finding wisdom from near and far. In doing so, as the lyricist Sting put it, "It seems I'm not alone in being alone."

May you, too, find yourself connected, challenged, and comforted by these wonderful words from the past and present.

FOREWORD

BUILDING A LIFE OF VALUE

The VALUES OF THE WISE series is a stellar collection of words of wisdom, witticisms, and reflections. These books provide a compelling fusion of progressive ideals grounded in classical values.

They deliver thousands of quotations from a diversity of writers, celebrities, philosophers, politicians—the knowns and unknowns from classical to contemporary times. They bring centuries of wise thought from every corner of the world together in one complete set. Sometimes amusing, sometimes poignant, they always present an honest look at life that will enlighten, challenge, and inspire you.

Many of the most profound thoughts on record are in these timeless volumes. The casual reader will frequently find them amusing and will almost always learn something from them. The more serious researcher of wisdom and humanity will certainly gain greater self-knowledge, direction, and true inspiration in their pages. Whatever your purpose in picking them up, these books connect us with others who have pondered life's meaning and stimulate an internal intellectual dialogue with them. Because of this, they can also be a resource for your deep personal journey in living *a life of value.*

These volumes uniquely combine humane and humanistic principles and ideals into a transcultural fusion of classical and progressive values. These engaging and inspirational books are wonderful additions to the library or coffee table of anyone seeking to understand and honor the virtues that have been sought by the wise and visionary throughout history, from diverse walks of life, representing many cultures and perspectives.

From ready reference to a stimulus for profound introspection, the VALUES OF THE WISE books illuminate humanity's highest aspirations.

CHAPTER ONE

KNOWLEDGE, WISDOM, & EDUCATION

Wisdom is really a way of thinking, an ability to see beyond what something is to what it *represents*. It requires a distinct openness to experience. It allows us to process things at a level that gives us a deeper understanding of *what is what*, if you will. Partisan political feelings and an inflexible belief about God are examples of the fact that if we close our minds to certain ideas and perspectives, we may be experiencing some convincing substitute for wisdom. Hesitancy and doubt mark the pursuit of wisdom. Because not all ideas and beliefs have equal merit, a person pursuing wisdom tries to distill all the knowledge and facts surrounding them down to the richest points and most important lessons. And then hold onto that belief modestly! It can be a challenge to grasp the difference between knowledge and wisdom. I think of it like this: knowledge may be right or wrong (such as the shape of the earth), but wisdom is always true. It has also been said that wisdom may not be used for evil purposes. How does one transform knowledge into wisdom? Peter Abelard offers a guideline: "The first key to wisdom is this – constant and frequent questioning…for by doubting we are led to question and by questioning we arrive at the truth." It takes a brave person to pursue virtues such as justice, truth, and honor – and the wiser one becomes, the clearer they become. Thomas Aquinas, an ancient pursuer of wisdom, remarked on the value of this lifelong quest: "Of all the pursuits open to men, the search for wisdom is more perfect, more sublime, more profitable, and more full of joy."

The noblest pleasure is the joy of understanding.

— *Leonardo da Vinci*   1

JASON A. MERCHEY

The highest result of education is tolerance.

— *HELEN KELLER*

The teacher is like the farmer or the physician. The farmer doesn't produce the grains of the field; he merely helps them grow. The physician does not produce the health of the body; he merely helps the body maintain its health or regain its health. And the teacher does not produce knowledge in the mind; he merely helps the mind discover it for itself.

— *MORTIMER J. ADLER*

What we need to know, we already know. It is not more knowledge that is needed, but more careful listening, more dreaming, more daring.

— *JAN PHILLIPS*

As the water shapes itself to the vessel that contains it, so a wise man adapts himself to circumstances.

— *CONFUCIUS*

I've not only used all the brains I have,
but all that I can borrow.

— *WOODROW WILSON*

My parents struggled to give us a college education… Father always talked to us about having a choice in life, and he said an education would give us that choice.

— *SARA MARTÍNEZ TUCKER*

Let me embrace thee, sour adversity, for wise men say it is the wisest course.

— *WILLIAM SHAKESPEARE*

CHAPTER

ONE

In the final analysis, it is not what you do for your children, but what you have taught them to do for themselves that will make them successful human beings.

— ANN LANDERS

The end of all education should surely be service to others. We cannot seek achievement for ourselves and forget about the progress and prosperity of our community. Our ambitions must be broad enough to include the aspirations and needs of others for their sake and for our own.

— CESAR CHAVEZ

Now, thousands of years later, when we are nearing the possibility of a second social transformation – this time a shift from a dominator society to a more advanced version of a partnership society – we need to understand everything we can about this astonishing piece of our lost past. For at stake at this second evolutionary crossroads, when we possess the technologies of total destruction once attributed only to God, may be nothing less than the survival of our species.

— RIANE EISLER

The history of a nation is, unfortunately, too easily written as the history of its dominant class.

— KWAME NKRUMAH

Philosophy will clip an angel's wings,
Conquer all mysteries by rule and line,
Empty the haunted air, and gnomed mine –
Unweave a rainbow.

— JOHN KEATS

He has a first-rate mind until he makes it up.

— VIOLET BONHAM CARTER

Only two kinds of people can attain self-knowledge: those who are not encumbered at all with learning, that is to say, whose minds are not overcrowded with thoughts borrowed from others; and those who, after studying all the scriptures and sciences, have come to realize that they know nothing.

— RAMAKRISHNA PARAMAHAMSADEVA

To write is to descend, to excavate, to go underground.

— ANAIS NIN

Men are idolaters, and want something to look at and kiss and hug, or throw themselves down before; they always did, they always will, and if you don't make it out of wood, you must make it out of words.

— OLIVER WENDELL HOLMES

Calculate what man knows and it cannot compare to what he does not know.

— CHUANG TZU

Experience is a good teacher, but she sends in terrific bills.

— MINNA ANTRIM

The roots of education are bitter, but the fruits are sweet.

— ARISTOTLE

It is good to know the truth, but better to speak of palm trees.

— ARABIC PROVERB

It's not what you thought,
When you first began it.
You got what you want,
Now you can hardly stand it.
By now you know,
It's not going to stop until you wise up.

— AIMEE MANN

CHAPTER

ONE

When the press is free, and every man is able to read, all is safe.
— *Thomas Jefferson*

In the process of becoming educated we learn from each other
and, in so doing, we destroy the barriers that separate us from
one another; we demolish prejudices that impede us from
becoming fully human.
— *Francisco Jiménez*

The only thing we learn from history is that we do not learn.
— *Earl Warren*

Learning without wisdom is a load of books on a donkey's back.
— *Zora Neale Hurston*

We live in the present, we dream of the future,
but we learn eternal truths from the past.
— *Chiang Kai-shek*

Never be afraid to sit awhile and think.
— *Lorraine Hansberry*

A good listener is not only popular everywhere, but
after a while he gets to know something.
— *Wilson Mizner*

From the stars and the sun and the moon man should learn.
— *Eagle Chief*

The modern era, dedicated to repeatable experimental data,
buried something valuable that cannot be resurrected by
scientific language: namely, the qualities of knowing that rely
on unification between an observer and the object observed.
— *Helen Palmer*

Wherever they burn books, they will also, in the end, burn human beings.
— *HEINRICH HEINE*

A wise man hears one word but understands two.
— *JEWISH PROVERB*

If we would have new knowledge, we must get a whole world of new questions.
— *SUSANNE K. LANGER*

To believe everything is to be an imbecile.
To deny everything is to be a fool.
— *CHARLES NODIER*

Like the bee gathering honey from different flowers, the wise man accepts the essence of different Scriptures and sees only the good in all religions.
— *SRIMAD BHAGAVATAM*

A mind always in contact with children and servants, whose aspirations and ambitions rise no higher than the roof that shelters them, is necessarily dwarfed in its proportions.
— *ELIZABETH CADY STANTON*

Reason is the greatest enemy faith has.
— *MARTIN LUTHER*

The principle of *utility* requires that we do not take refuge in ideological slogans, cultural traditions, or personal opinion, but that we instead examine our position on various moral issues in light of the actual consequences. This entails overcoming our ignorance regarding the extent to which our lifestyle is built upon the suffering of other people or animals.
— *JUDITH A. BOSS*

There is no darkness but ignorance.

— *WILLIAM SHAKESPEARE*

You live and learn. At any rate, you live.

— *DOUGLAS ADAMS*

The bitterness of studying is preferable to the
bitterness of ignorance.

— *PHILIPPINE PROVERB*

No one has yet fully realized the wealth of sympathy, kindness,
and generosity hidden in the soul of a child. The effort of every
true education should be to unlock that treasure.

— *EMMA GOLDMAN*

Wisdom cannot be bought for money.

— *OVAMBO PROVERB*

A school where you've got good character education is one
where the culture of the school puts a high premium on
respect, honesty, and kids being responsible for their actions
and adults doing the same.

— *ESTHER SCHAEFFER*

Knowledge was inherent in all things. The world was a library
and its books were the stones, leaves, grass, brooks...
We learned to do what only the students of nature ever learn,
and that was to feel beauty.

— *LUTHER STANDING BEAR*

Genius may have its limitations, but stupidity is not
thus handicapped.

— *ELBERT HUBBARD*

JASON A. MERCHEY

People are no longer sinful; they are only immature or
underprivileged or frightened or, more particularly, sick.

— *PHYLLIS MCGINLEY*

It is the mark of an educated mind to be able to
entertain a thought without accepting it.

— *ARISTOTLE*

As both Aristotle and Thomas Aquinas insisted, wisdom is to
be contrasted with cleverness because cleverness is the ability
to take right steps to any end, whereas wisdom is related
only to good ends.

— *PHILIPPA FOOT*

Teachers open the door, but you must enter by yourself.

— *CHINESE PROVERB*

Understanding the atom is a childish game in comparison
with the understanding of the childish game.

— *ALBERT EINSTEIN*

We have a hunger of the mind which asks for knowledge of all
around us; and the more we gain, the more is our desire.
The more we see, the more we are capable of seeing.

— *MARIA MITCHELL*

Books are preserved minds.

— *JAPANESE PROVERB*

What is so hard about just saying the words, "I don't know?
I – Don't – Know." Of course there are questions that plague
all of us: How did we get here? What happens when we die? Is
there a heaven? Am I on the list? Who let the dogs out? But
why would you believe some other human being whose brain
is no bigger or better than yours, I promise you, when he tells
you that he knows what happens when you die?

— *BILL MAHER*

CHAPTER

ONE

Wisdom involves exceptional breadth and depth of knowledge about the conditions of life and human affairs and reflective judgment about the application of this knowledge.

— *DEIRDRE A. KRAMER*

A little learning, indeed, may be a dangerous thing, but the want of learning is a calamity to any people.

— *FREDERICK DOUGLASS*

Winning the [Nobel] Prize [for physics] wasn't half as exciting as doing the work itself.

— *MARIA GOEPPERT MAYER*

A poem begins in delight and ends in wisdom.

— *ROBERT FROST*

Many still don't see any relationship between driving a large vehicle and global-warming gas emissions or rising consumption of paper and the loss of ancient forests. We must help people make these kinds of associations.

— *BETSY TAYLOR*

To learn the whole Talmud is a great accomplishment; to learn one good virtue is even greater.

— *YIDDISH PROVERB*

There is nothing more dangerous than ignorance being practiced.

— *JOHANN WOLFGANG VON GOETHE*

The rank and file are not philosophers, they are not educated to think for themselves, but simply to accept, unquestioned, whatever comes.

— *SUSAN B. ANTHONY*

JASON A. MERCHEY

Ignorance is not innocence, but sin.
— *ROBERT BROWNING*

Who is wise? – he who learns from all men.
— *THE TALMUD*

More mass media are controlled by fewer monolithic
corporations than ever before. The choices proliferate, and
yet there's little of substance to see or hear. In the midst
of abundance, we are starving for substance.
— *MICHAEL TOMS*

People do not like to think. If one thinks, one must reach
conclusions. Conclusions are not always pleasant.
— *HELEN KELLER*

It's bad taste to be wise all the time,
like being at a perpetual funeral.
— *D. H. LAWRENCE*

At the moment that you are most in awe of all there is about
life that you don't understand, you are closer to
understanding it all than at any other time.
— *JANE WAGNER*

Young men are apt to think themselves wise enough, as drunk
men are apt to think themselves sober enough.
— *LORD CHESTERFIELD*

All wisdom is not taught in your school.
— *HAWAIIAN PROVERB*

If you want to understand today, you have to search yesterday.
— *PEARL S. BUCK*

One's ears hear a lot; one's eyes see a lot. The wise person
should not believe everything seen or heard.

— *Siddhartha Gautama*

Knowledge was an addiction: once we had some, we wanted
more. The way we got it was through inquiry and toil.

— *Ray Suárez*

Better untaught than ill-taught.

— *English proverb*

Men and women must be educated, in great degree, by the
opinions and manners of the society they live in. In every
age there has been a stream of popular opinion that has
carried all before it, and given a family character, as it were,
to the century. It may then fairly be inferred, that, until society
be differently constituted, much cannot be expected
from education.

— *Mary Wollstonecraft*

Learning is a treasure that will follow its owner everywhere.

— *Chinese proverb*

We don't believe in rheumatism and true love
until after the first attack.

— *Marie Ebner von Eschenbach*

We are all geniuses up to the age of ten.

— *Aldous Huxley*

If there is an opinion, facts will be found to support it.

— *Judy Spoorles*

JASON A. MERCHEY

In the midst of the tears and shocked faces of New Yorkers, in
the midst of the lethal air we breathed as we worked at Ground
Zero, in the midst of my children's terror at being so close to
this crime against humanity, in the midst of all this, I held on to
a glimmer of hope in the naïve assumption that something
good could come out of it. And then came the speech:
You are either with us or against us.

— *TIM ROBBINS*

You can either be wise or you can have knowledge.
But you can't "know" wisdom. You have to "be" it.

— *RAM DASS*

Never mistake knowledge for wisdom – one helps you make
a living; the other helps you make a life.

— *SANDRA CAREY*

To be able to be caught up in the world of thought –
that is to be educated.

— *EDITH HAMILTON*

Recognition is the key to liberation.

— *TIBETAN PROVERB*

Poetic knowledge is born in the great silence
of scientific knowledge.

— *AIMÉ CÉSAIRE*

A little philosophy inclineth a man to atheism; but depth in
philosophy bringeth men's minds about to religion.

— *FRANCIS BACON*

The old love of life and nature and the old ways of sharing
rather than taking away, of caring for rather than oppressing,
and the view of power as responsibility rather than domination
did not die out. But like women and qualities associated with
femininity, they were relegated to a secondary place.

— *RIANE EISLER*

Each one thinks much of his own wisdom; therefore
the world is full of fools.

— *SWEDISH PROVERB*

If knowledge does not liberate the self from the self,
then ignorance is better than such knowledge.

— *HAKIM SANA'I*

I sincerely believe in the value of education – of attempting
to gain knowledge of whatever situation is leading to
feelings of anxiety.

— *SUE MCPHERSON*

To realize the unimportance of time is the gate of wisdom.

— *BERTRAND RUSSELL*

Better to build schoolrooms for the boy than cells for the man.

— *ELIZA COOK*

Life would be infinitely happier if we could only be born at the
age of eighty and gradually approach eighteen.

— *MARK TWAIN*

So great is the confusion of the world that comes
from coveting knowledge!

— *CHUANG TZU*

How freely we live life depends both on our political system
and on our vigilance in defending its liberties. How long we live
depends both on our genes and on the quality of our health
care. How well we live – that is, how thoughtfully, how nobly,
how virtuously, how joyously, how lovingly – depends both on
our philosophy and on the way we apply it to all else. The
examined life is a better life....

— *LOU MARINOFF*

JASON A. MERCHEY

Theory is often contrasted with action. This is a false
dichotomy, since it is theory that informs our actions.
— *JUDITH A. BOSS*

It takes a clever man to turn cynic, and a wise man to
be clever enough not to.
— *FANNIE HURST*

Against reason, no sword will prevail.
— *JAPANESE PROVERB*

I've been horribly educated, history-wise – and otherwise.
There are glaring holes in my general knowledge of the world.
I don't pretend to know what I don't, but I sure wish I knew
more, and am pretty consistently working to
make sure that's the case.
— *HALLIE SMITH*

Results! Why man, I have gotten a lot of results.
I know 50,000 things that won't work.
— *THOMAS A. EDISON*

Only people who die very young learn all they really
need to know in kindergarten.
— *WENDY KAMINER*

The fundamental test for the relevance of higher learning is
whether its overarching mission and the questions considered
do not shirk the examination of values that inhere in reality,
and especially in the social reality we make through our social
relationships and institutions.
— *MARCUS G. RASKIN*

How do I know the universe is like this? By looking!
— *LAO TZU*

> I never believed that I was imposing my views on blank slates,
> on innocent minds. My students had a long period of political
> indoctrination before they arrived in my class – in the family, in
> high school, in the mass media. Into a marketplace so long
> dominated by orthodoxy I wanted only to wheel my little
> pushcart, offering my wares along with the others, leaving
> students to make their own choices.
>
> — *HOWARD ZINN*

True education is not limited to the classroom – we learn from our everyday experiences, our interactions with others, from going to a museum, chatting with someone, or even reading the comics. Parents have a huge opportunity to educate their children, but oftentimes it takes a back seat to television or video games or problems going on in the home. Learning is so craved by humans that children are intent on barraging the world with questions and exploration. Yet by the time most children reach adolescence, that once-insatiable sense of curiosity is replaced by apathy, as they sit in the classroom slumped in their chairs, repeating to themselves something like, "This teacher is a moron," "This subject is so stupid," or "Why am I even here?" I believe this is more than just age-based rebelliousness: something fundamental is wrong. Our public education system is in dire need of invigoration and reformation. Education is natural, fun, and profitable; it is one of the paths that lead to knowledge, and possibly to wisdom. What can we do to keep the flame of desire for knowledge alive? Instead of teaching children simply to tow the line, let's teach them to think critically, to act independently, and to challenge authority wisely. Education is about drawing out the potential within a child; it comes from the Latin word *educare*, meaning "to draw out." We would see the majority of our national and planetary problems ease if we were to rethink and prioritize education in a way that honors the wonders it possesses.

RESPECT, TOLERANCE, & MODESTY

When I went to summer camp at age 13, the counselor had only one rule: to show respect. This was rather different from the "list of 10 rules" that was posted in my elementary school classrooms up to that time. This new idea – that respect was so powerful that it encompassed all other rules, was a first-class education in respect. Sure, there was a greater feeling of freedom from authority. But I am clear that the inevitable disagreements, shenanigans, and "bad behavior" that resulted from putting ten boys together in a cabin for three weeks without parental supervision could be viewed from the perspective of respect. This was always an important concept for me as I went on a few years later to work with children, and I haven't stopped doing so since. Respect for others is not easy to have sometimes, but I urge you to remember that you don't "lose" anything (like you lose money) by giving it. It is more than just being courteous and deferent to elders; one can show respect to a homeless person by looking them straight in the face as he or she walks by, or simply by saying "excuse me" if you behave badly. The poet Kahlil Gibran's wonderful thought on the way to treat even the youngest and least powerful people is the oldest quotation I remember: "Keep me away from the wisdom which does not want, the joy which does not weep, and the greatness which does not bow before children."

Speak softly but carry a big stick.

— *WEST AFRICAN PROVERB*

JASON A. MERCHEY

You can't have conflict resolution without conflict. Both on the
international level and in my own bedroom, I have found that
if you either fix it too fast or try to avoid it, you will never reach
resolution. You have to learn to dance with conflict and to
transform it. When you do that, you can have resolution.

— *DANAAN PARRY*

No one can persuade another to change. Each of us guards
a gate of change that can only be opened from the inside.
We cannot open the gate of another, either by argument
or by emotional appeal.

— *MARILYN FERGUSON*

Happiness is a butterfly, which, when pursued, is always just
beyond your grasp, but which, if you will sit down quietly,
may alight upon you.

— *NATHANIEL HAWTHORNE*

The only title in our democracy superior to that of the
President is the title of citizen.

— *LOUIS BRANDEIS*

With compassion, we see benevolently our own human
condition and the condition of our fellow beings.
We drop prejudice. We withhold judgment.

— *CHRISTINA BALDWIN*

He who becomes arrogant with wealth and power...
sows the seeds of his own misfortune.

— *LAO TZU*

It is important to recognize that our achievements not only
speak well for us, they speak well for those persons and forces,
seen, unseen, and unnoticed, that have been active in our lives.

— *ANNE WILSON SCHAEF*

My parents shared not only an improbable love; they shared an abiding faith in the possibilities of this nation. They would give me an African name, Barack, or "blessed," believing that in a tolerant America your name is no barrier to success.

— *BARACK OBAMA*

The Christians are right: it is pride which has been the chief cause of misery in every nation and every family since the world began.

— *C. S. LEWIS*

There is nothing noble about being superior to some other person. True nobility is in being superior to your previous self.

— *HINDUSTANI PROVERB*

Understanding a person does not mean condoning; it only means that one does not accuse him as if one were God or a judge placed above him.

— *ERICH FROMM*

One cannot collect all the beautiful shells on the beach.

— *ANNE MORROW LINDBERGH*

Men never do evil so cheerfully and so completely as when they do so from religious conviction.

— *BLAISE PASCAL*

To be uncertain is to be uncomfortable, but to be certain is ridiculous.

— *CHINESE PROVERB*

Modesty is the gentle art of enhancing your charm by pretending not to be aware of it.

— *OLIVER HERFORD*

JASON A. MERCHEY

The opposite of talking isn't listening.
The opposite of talking is waiting.
— FRAN LEBOWITZ

Be nice to people on your way up because you might
meet them on your way down.
— JIMMY DURANTE

Without feelings of respect, what is there to distinguish
men from beasts?
— CONFUCIUS

Let Greeks be Greeks, and women what they are.
— ANNE BRADSTREET

Praise shames me, for I secretly beg for it.
— RABINDRANATH TAGORE

In the end, I'm never satisfied that I have a complete
understanding of any problem.
— MICHAEL E. KERR

Toleration…is the greatest gift of the mind; it requires the same
effort of the brain that it takes to balance oneself on a bicycle.
— HELEN KELLER

Modesty is the only bait when you angle for praise.
— LORD CHESTERFIELD

I didn't pull myself up by my bootstraps, I had a lot
of help from my family.
— ELOY RODRÍGUEZ

TWO

One of the basic causes for all the trouble in the world today
is that people talk too much and think too little. They act
impulsively without thinking. I always try to think before I talk.

— *MARGARET CHASE SMITH*

Biologically, we are saying that race is no longer
a valid distinction.

— *SOLOMON H. KATZ*

He who wants a rose must respect the thorn.

— *PERSIAN PROVERB*

I believe that too many people put themselves above the Earth,
like it belongs to them. We are part of it all, not better than any
other living thing. We as a society tend to believe that we can
control the happenings on this earth, forgetting that we "own"
nothing and we are simply here to be part of nature and help
and enjoy it. Too many of us are disconnected from the Earth's
beauty and magic...and I believe that is at the root of our most
pressing problems.

— *KERRI BORDAK*

What's done to children, they will do to society.

— *KARL MENNINGER*

If each of us goes to the Holy Book, I don't think
we'll ever reach a solution.

— *PRINCE SAUD AL-FAISAL*

True patriotism doesn't exclude an understanding
of the patriotism of others.

— *QUEEN ELIZABETH II*

JASON A. MERCHEY

To be simple is the best thing in the world; to be modest is the
next best thing. I am not sure about being quiet.
— *G. K. Chesterton*

We habitually erect a barrier called blame that keeps us from
communicating genuinely with others, and we fortify it with
our concepts of who's right and who's wrong.
— *Pema Chödrön*

The world is made up for the most part of morons and natural
tyrants, sure of themselves, strong in their own opinions, never
doubting anything.
— *Clarence Darrow*

If you suffer pain, anxiety, ambition, soon you don't know what
love is. You want to have power, position, better house, better
cars. Have you ever understood that a man who is ambitious
has no love in his heart?
— *Jiddu Krishnamurti*

If anyone would like to acquire humility, I can, I think, tell
them the first step. The first step is to realize that one is proud.
And a big step too. At least, nothing whatever can be done
before it. If you think you are not conceited, it means you are
very conceited indeed.
— *C. S. Lewis*

Most conversations are simply monologues delivered
in the presence of witnesses.
— *Margaret Millar*

Honest disagreement is often a good sign of progress.
— *Mohandas K. Gandhi*

TWO CHAPTER

If you're trying to show off for other people, forget it. They will look down on you anyhow. And if you're trying to show off for people at the bottom, forget it. They will only envy you. Status will get you nowhere.

— *MORRIE SCHWARTZ*

Fortune does not change men, it unmasks them.

— *SUZANNE NECKER*

Do not condemn the judgment of another because it differs from your own. You may both be wrong.

— *DANDEMIS*

The trouble with the world is that the stupid are cocksure and the intelligent are full of doubt.

— *BERTRAND RUSSELL*

All too often, visions of virtue or decency have been invoked to brand as immoral and dangerous anyone who is different. Such aggressive moral dogmatism – which, it is worth stressing, can occur on both the political right and left – is one of the greatest enemies of human dignity.

— *ELIZABETH KISS*

In the practice of tolerance, one's enemy is the best teacher.

— *TENZIN GYATSO*

There will be no peace if there is no justice...no justice if there is no equity...no equity if there is no progress...no progress if there is no democracy...no democracy if there is no respect for the identity and dignity of the peoples and cultures in today's world.

— *RIGOBERTA MENCHU*

JASON A. MERCHEY

Whatever accomplishment you boast of in the world,
there is someone better than you.

— *African Proverb*

Few, save the poor, feel for the poor.

— *Letitia Elizabeth Landon*

There must be civil disobedience of laws which are contrary to
human welfare. But there must be also an uncompromising
practice of treating everyone, including the worst of our
opponents, with all the respect and decency that he merits as a
fellow human being. We can expect to face tear gas, clubs and
bullets. But we must refuse to hate, punish or kill in return...

— *Dave Dellinger*

I've looked at life from both sides now,
From win and lose, and still somehow,
It's life's illusions I recall.
I really don't know life at all.

— *Joni Mitchell*

There is a sufficiency in the world for man's need but
not for man's greed.

— *Mohandas K. Gandhi*

The love of our neighbor in all its fullness simply means being
able to say to him, "What are you going through?"

— *Simone Weil*

None who have always been free can understand the terrible
fascinating power of the hope of freedom to those
who are not free.

— *Pearl S. Buck*

TWO

Let us be a little humble; let us think that the truth
may not perhaps be entirely with us.

— *Jawaharlal Nehru*

Each time the United States becomes imperial it betrays
the very keystone upon which its greatness rests.

— *Anna Quindlen*

Modesty is the art of encouraging people to find out for
themselves how wonderful you are.

— *Anonymous*

Respect is carried not in great, bold proclamations, but in small
moments of surprising intimacy and empathy.

— *Sara Lawrence-Lightfoot*

It is better to be ignorant than to be mistaken.

— *Japanese proverb*

Let women only acquire knowledge and humanity, and love will
teach them modesty.

— *Mary Wollstonecraft*

I do not have a Pollyanna view of human nature. I am quite
aware that out of defensiveness and inner fear, individuals can
and do behave in ways which are incredibly cruel, horribly
destructive, immature, regressive, anti-social, and harmful. Yet
one of the most refreshing parts of my experience is to work
with such individuals and to discover the strongly positive
directional tendencies which exist in all of them,
as in all of us, at the deepest levels.

— *Carl Rogers*

JASON A. MERCHEY

We do not inherit the earth from our ancestors,
we borrow it from our children.

— *HAIDA PROVERB*

I'm just a person trapped inside a woman's body.

— *ROBIN MORGAN*

Whoever kindles the flame of intolerance in America
is lighting a fire underneath his own home.

— *HAROLD E. STASSEN*

The best of alms is that which the right hand gives,
and the left hand knows it not.

— *MUHAMMAD*

My God, what do we want? What does any human being want?
Take away an accident of pigmentation of a thin layer of our
outer skin and there is no difference between me and
anyone else. All we want is for that trivial difference to
make no difference.

— *SHIRLEY CHISHOLM*

The historical record of religions on tolerance is
drenched in the blood of intolerance.

— *CHARLES PANATI*

Do nothing to others which, if done to you,
would cause you pain.

— *THE MAHABHARATA*

Whether they are defending the Soviet Union or bleating for
Saddam Hussein, liberals are always against America. They are
either traitors or idiots, and on the matter of America's
self-preservation, the difference is irrelevant. Fifty years
of treason hasn't slowed them down.

— *ANN COULTER*

CHAPTER

Money is also welcome because it enables you on many occasions to help other people. But any ostentatious display is something I don't like.

— *PLÁCIDO DOMINGO*

I would no more quarrel with a man because of his religion than I would because of his art.

— *MARY BAKER EDDY*

Much of the insensibility and hardness of the world is due to the lack of imagination which prevents a realization of the experience of other people.

— *JANE ADDAMS*

Human beings are in many ways special; and an adequate morality must acknowledge that. But it is also true that we are only one species among many inhabiting this planet; and morality must acknowledge that as well.

— *JAMES RACHELS*

Racist, sexist, and homophobic thoughts cannot, alas, be abolished by fate, but only by the time-honored methods of persuasion, education, and exposure to the other guy's – or excuse me – woman's, point of view.

— *BARBARA EHRENREICH*

Don't ever take a fence down until you know why it was put up.

— *ROBERT FROST*

There are many specific ways for the United States to rebuild its relations with the world. It can match its military buildup with diplomatic efforts that demonstrate its interest and engagement in the world's problems. But above all, it must make the world comfortable with its power by leading through consensus.

— *FAREED ZAKARIA*

27

The simple fact is that our current unsustainable, "more-is-better" culture undermines any hope of achieving justice – at home or abroad. We often hear about how the United States consumes a vastly disproportionate amount of resources relative to the rest of the world. Americans are building bigger houses, driving bigger cars, and consuming more and more of everything than just about anyone else anywhere.

— NYDIA M. VELÁZQUEZ

Think of your fellow men and women as holy people who were put here by the Great Spirit. Think of being related to all things.

— ED MCGAA

Everyone has bad stretches and real successes.
Either way, you have to be careful not to lose your confidence or get too confident.

— NANCY KERRIGAN

If you try to cleanse others, you will waste away like soap in the process.

— MADAGASCAN PROVERB

Success has made failures of many men.

— CINDY ADAMS

I had to ask myself some very hard questions. I prided myself on being open-minded, non-racist, non-sexist; so how could I be afraid of people I knew nothing about?

— LEAH GREEN

Many prophets of the major religions were themselves remarkably open-minded. Jesus Christ surrounded himself with society's outcasts. Often it has been the followers of the prophets who, to consolidate power, honed the sharp sword of intolerance.

— CHARLES PANATI

CHAPTER TWO

You grow up the day you have the first real laugh at yourself.
— *ETHEL BARRYMORE*

The only alternative to coexistence is codestruction.
— *JAWAHARLAL NEHRU*

It is a wholesome and necessary thing for us to turn again to
the earth and in the contemplation of her beauties to know
of wonder and humility.
— *RACHEL CARSON*

Censure not, pious man, in the purity of your soul, the lover
of wine, for in your book of account will not be written the
sins of others.
— *HAFIZ*

What I want to see is the demise of fundamentalism in favor of
pragmatism. By fundamentalism I mean any philosophy that
thinks it has the final and unique answer, that believes that
there is one essential plan underlying the workings of the
universe, and that seeks to make sure everyone else gets
persuaded to fall in line with it.
— *BRIAN ENO*

We deny the right of any portion of the species to decide for
another what is and what is not their "proper sphere." The
proper sphere for all human beings is the largest
and highest which they are able to attain.
— *HARRIET TAYLOR*

He that is without sin among you, let him cast the first stone.
— *JESUS OF NAZARETH*

JASON A. MERCHEY

Real kindness is mouth-gaping respect and compassion for just
how hard it is to be a human being – any human being.

— *REBECCA ALBAN HOFFBERGER*

After listening to thousands of pleas for pardon to offenders,
I can hardly recall a case where I did not feel that I might have
fallen as my fellow man had done, if I had been subjected
to the same demoralizing influences and pressed
by the same temptations.

— *HORATIO SEYMOUR*

The reduction of nonhuman animals and the environment
to the status of resources for humans has had a devastating
effect on the environment.

— *JUDITH A. BOSS*

Accepting uncertainty as our philosophy might allow us to
honor each other's stories more, delighting in all the bizarre
and wondrous interpretations of the mystery. We might also
show more tolerance for those who appear to be fools
and for those who speak truths we don't wish to hear.

— *WES NISKER*

How do we create a harmonious society out of so many kinds
of people? The key is tolerance – the one value that is
indispensable in creating community.

— *BARBARA JORDAN*

I find it utterly impossible to observe another animal without
seeing it as a kindred being, a bearer and representative of life
just as I am, and in this respect wholly equal to myself...
Though I differ in many ways from other living entities,
I cannot feel that there is any ontological superiority
in my being human.

— *IRVING SINGER*

It's a fact that people can change only if they feel they are
basically liked and accepted as they are. When people feel
criticized, disliked, and unappreciated, they are unable
to change. Instead, they feel under siege and dig in
to protect themselves.

— *JOHN GOTTMAN & NAN SILVER*

Recognize yourselves in he or she who are not like you or me.

— *CARLOS FUENTES*

It's perfectly understandable to discover the roots of your
religion and want to share it with everyone you meet. By the
same token, please understand the basic tenets of my religion,
which specifically proscribe that: should you knock on my door,
corner me on an elevator, or sit next to me on a flight
yammering on and on about how your way is the right way,
I am morally obligated by the elders of my church to
tell you to shut the &#@* up.

— *DENNIS MILLER*

A strong community will include people of different ages,
ethnic backgrounds, socioeconomic statuses, and interests.
Community, communication, and communion all come from
the same word, meaning "together" and "next to." Embedded
in the world is the concept of shared place.

— *MARY PIPHER*

The right time to show your good character is when you
are pestered by somebody weaker than you.

— *SIDDHARTHA GAUTAMA*

Unlike Hinduism and most Western ethics, Buddhism is
nonhierarchical, emphasizing oneness and the interrelatedness
and moral value of all living beings. Right living, therefore,
includes compassion and an attitude of nonviolence
toward all of nature.

— *JUDITH A. BOSS*

JASON A. MERCHEY

Responsibility could easily deteriorate into domination and possessiveness were it not for respect...respect means the concern that the other person should grow and unfold as he is.

— *ERICH FROMM*

One should not pry into the faults of others, what they've done and left undone. Consider instead what you yourself have done and left undone.

— *SIDDHARTHA GAUTAMA*

One time I got a letter from a woman complaining about some people who had just moved in next door. There was a guy with long hair and a couple of women with short hair. It was clear from her letter that these were gay people, and she wasn't happy about having them move into her nice neighborhood. She said, "We're disgusted with these types. What can we do to improve the neighborhood?" My answer was, "You could move."

— *ABIGAIL VAN BUREN*

Socrates said, "Those who want the fewest things are nearest to the gods."

— *DIOGENES*

Modesty is a fascinating idea that each of us has countless opportunities to bring to life. It is borne of a certain confidence, "classiness," and understatement. It is akin to respect, in that they both involve a kind of deference or discipline, with respect being more about the other and modesty being relatively about the self. I remember when I was a child, I was a mediocre soccer player. I had awe and admiration for a teammate named Sean, who possessed a lot of practiced skill in the game. I recall that he would make a goal and have an absolutely expressionless face – no gloating or grandstanding. He would just get back down to business and immediately take up his position downfield. However, when I made a goal it was cause for exultant, arms-in-the-air celebration! I believe this is because Sean had modesty and I didn't. Why?

TWO

Probably not just because his father the coach made sure to teach him a sense of respecting his opponents by abstaining from showing off, but more importantly, because Sean *knew* he was good. He was excellent. And it is almost as though his scoring a goal was no surprise to him, and thus, no elation. Me – when I scored a goal, which conflicted with my self-image of "crappy soccer player," it was a remarkable occurrence. I'm not convinced that Sean is any better overall, or any happier in his adulthood than I am. But he did exemplify modesty as a child, and I am now studying it as an adult. Enjoy these wonderful, old ideas.

FULFILLMENT, MEANING, & OPTIMISM

Optimism is a deliberate and beneficial way of thinking that arms the chooser with a positive mindset. It is a "faithful" attitude: faith in the fact that a difficult situation is likely to go well. It is seeing the proverbial glass of water as being half-full rather than half-empty, and it works well in situations where you can endure the possibility of failure. Thus, optimism applies to "small things" *and* to huge, life-changing situations as well. Optimism and hope are a wellspring of energy to keep the flame within the heart of humankind; they conjure up a spirit of positive expectations and an unwillingness to yield that at one time led us out of the jungle – and to the moon. Fulfillment is part of *a life of value* because it means joy, comfort, and "a filling up of one's self." Your life cannot be entirely about service, determination, and effort – that would be valuable to the world but would be missing out on so much of the engrossing and wonderful experiences that the word *fulfillment* captures. This exciting chapter presents diverse thoughts on the virtue of asking that girl out, applying for a new job, and doing something that matters.

Most of us have jobs that are too small for our spirits.

— STUDS TERKEL

JASON A. MERCHEY

The best-educated human being is the one who understands
the most about the life in which he is placed.

— HELEN KELLER

I'd like to live like a poor man with lots of money.

— PABLO PICASSO

I have now reigned about fifty years in victory or peace, beloved
by my subjects, dreaded by my enemies, and respected by my
allies. Riches and honors, power and pleasure, have waited on
my call. Nor does any earthly pleasure appear to have been
wanting to my felicity. In this situation I have diligently
numbered the days of pure and genuine happiness which have
fallen to my lot. They amount to fourteen.

— ABD-ER-RAHMAN III

As the American spirit teeters between rage and compassion,
pray we tip toward compassion and take the world with us.

— GERALDINE LAYBOURNE

When you find the person you want to spend the rest of
your life with, you want the rest of your life to start
as soon as possible.

— NORA EPHRON

The clearest way into the universe is through
a forest wilderness.

— JOHN MUIR

Our mounting global problems are in large part the logical
consequences of a "dominator" model of social organization at
our level of technological development – and hence can not be
solved within it. They also show that there is another course
which, as co-creators of our own evolution, is still ours to
choose. This is the alternative of breakthrough rather than
breakdown: how through new ways of structuring politics,
economics, science, and spirituality we can move into the
new era of a "partnership" world.

— RIANE EISLER

FULFILLMENT, MEANING, & OPTIMISM

CHAPTER THREE

Yes, there is a Nirvana; it is leading your sheep to a green pasture, and in putting your child to sleep, and in writing the last line of your poem.

— KAHLIL GIBRAN

As a day well-spent brings a happy sleep, so a life well used brings happy death.

— LEONARDO DA VINCI

Where, unwilling, dies the rose, Buds the new, another year.

— DOROTHY PARKER

God never meant to make life easy, he meant to make humans great.

— AUTHOR UNKNOWN

...everything on the earth has a purpose, every disease an herb to cure it, and every person a mission. This is the Indian theory of existence.

— MOURNING DOVE

The seduction of war is insidious because so much of what we are told about it is true; It does create a sense of comradeship, which obliterates our alienation and makes us, for perhaps the only time of our life, feel we belong. War allows us to rise above our small stations in life. We find nobility in a cause and feelings of selflessness and even bliss. And at a time of soaring deficits and financial scandals and the very deterioration of our domestic fabric, war is a fine diversion. War, for those who enter into combat, has a dark beauty, filled with the monstrous and the grotesque. The Bible calls it the "lust of the eye" and warns believers against it. War gives us a distorted sense of self; it gives us meaning.

— CHRIS HEDGES

37

JASON A. MERCHEY

Nothing contributes so much to tranquilize the mind
as a steady purpose – a point on which the soul may
fix its intellectual eye.

— MARY WOLLENSTONECRAFT

If thou covet riches, ask not but for contentment,
which is an immense treasure.

— SA'DI

Heaven knows how to put a proper price upon its goods;
and it would be strange indeed, if so celestial an article
as Freedom should not be highly rated.

— THOMAS PAINE

Alone, alone, oh! We have been warned about solitary vices.
Have solitary pleasures ever been adequately praised?
Do many people know that they exist?

— JESSAMYN WEST

I have faith in humankind, and it is this faith that has
allowed me to remain an active optimist.

— MIKHAIL GORBACHEV

People don't expect government to solve all their problems.
But they sense, deep in their bones, that with just a change in
priorities, we can make sure that every child in America has a
decent shot at life, and that the doors of opportunity remain
open to all. They know we can do better.

— BARACK OBAMA

We are discussing no small matter, but how we ought to live.

— SOCRATES

THREE

Like many others, in the aftermath of 9/11, I felt the country's
unity. I don't remember anything quite like it. I supported the
decision to enter Afghanistan and I hoped that the seriousness
of the times would bring forth strength, humility, and
wisdom in our leaders.

— *BRUCE SPRINGSTEEN*

And forget not that the earth delights to feel your bare feet
and the winds long to play with your hair.

— *KAHLIL GIBRAN*

In spite of everything, I still believe that people really are good
at heart. I simply can't build up my hopes on a foundation
consisting of confusion, misery, and death. I see the world
gradually being turned into a wilderness, I hear the ever-
approaching thunder, which will destroy us too, I can feel the
suffering of millions, and yet, if I look up into the heavens,
I think that it will all come right, that this cruelty will end,
and that peace and tranquility will return again.

— *ANNE FRANK*

I have often reflected upon the new vistas that reading opened
up to me. As I see it today, the ability to read awoke in me
some long-dormant craving to be mentally alive.

— *MALCOLM X*

It's a sad world, a very sad world; but I'm an optimist.

— *GOLDA MEIR*

Finding meaning in one's avocation, one's pursuit – consists of
determining what one's special area of intelligence or intrigue
is, and marrying that to the engine of passion to fuel its motion
as though one was finding a pleasing racetrack and flooring
the gas pedal.

— *JASON MERCHEY*

JASON A. MERCHEY

The more complete one's life is, the more...one's creative
capacities are fulfilled, the less one fears death...
People are not afraid of death per se, but of the
incompleteness of their own lives.

— LISA MARBURG GOODMAN

Art slows time and provides a break from capitalistic
competition and technological overkill – a break in which
we can ponder our lives, adjust our hearts, and pursue
a more meaningful existence.

— THOMAS HOLDER

I can't mate in captivity.

— GLORIA STEINEM

Grandfather, look at our brokenness.
We know that in all creation only the human family
has strayed from the Sacred Way.
We know that we are the ones who are divided, and we are the
ones who must come back together to walk in the Sacred Way.
Grandfather, Sacred One, teach us love, compassion, and
honor that we may heal the earth and heal each other.

— OJIBWA PRAYER

It is always darkest just before the day dawneth.

— THOMAS FULLER

Dream of a world where we measure character by how much we
share and care, not by how much we take and consume.

— JESSE JACKSON

We need wilderness whether or not we ever set foot in it. We
need a refuge even though we may never need to go there...
We need the possibility of escape as surely as we need hope.

— EDWARD ABBEY

THREE

My study of the history of religion has revealed that human beings are spiritual animals. Indeed, there is a case for arguing that *Homo sapiens* is also *Homo religious*. Men and women started to worship gods as soon as they became recognizably human; they created religions at the same time as they created works of art. This was not simply because they wanted to propitiate powerful forces; these early faiths expressed the wonder and mystery that seem always to have been an essential component of the human experience of this beautiful yet terrifying world. Like art, religion has been an attempt to find meaning and value in life, despite the suffering that flesh is heir to.

— *KAREN ARMSTRONG*

We can never finally know. I simply believe that some part of the human self or soul is not subject to the laws of space and time.

— *CARL JUNG*

People wish to be poets more than they wish to write poetry, and that's a mistake. One should wish to celebrate more than one wishes to be celebrated.

— *LUCILLE CLIFTON*

I always say that death can be one of the greatest experiences ever. If you live each day of your life right, then you have nothing to fear.

— *ELISABETH KÜBLER-ROSS*

Happiness is the only sanction in life; where happiness fails, existence remains a mad and lamentable experiment.

— *GEORGE SANTYANA*

I felt shelter to speak to you.

— *EMILY DICKINSON*

41

JASON A. MERCHEY

I was born upon the prairie, where the wind blew free, and
there was nothing to break the light of the sun. I was born
where there were no enclosures, and where everything drew
a free breath... I know every stream and every wood between
the Rio Grande and the Arkansas. I have hunted and lived over
that country. I lived like my fathers before me,
and like them, I lived happily.

— *Ten Bears*

I only regret that I have but one life to give for my country.

— *Nathan Hale*

Christ has no body now on earth but yours; yours are the only
hands with which he can do his work, yours are the only feet
with which he can go about the world, yours are the only eyes
through which his compassion can shine forth upon a troubled
world. Christ has no body on earth now but yours.

— *Teresa of Avila*

I have learned that success is measured not so much by the
position one has achieved in life as by the obstacles
he has overcome.

— *Booker T. Washington*

If we begin by being, then everything we do will
encompass...our whole self. When having is the impetus [for
our work], then the doing is influenced by material concerns,
which can never enable us to live our passion. One reason so
many people are dissatisfied and unhappy with their work is
that they begin by seeing to have rather than to be.

— *Justine Willis Toms & Michael Toms*

Life was not meant to be easy, my child; but take courage:
it can be delightful.

— *George Bernard Shaw*

CHAPTER

THREE

If we had no winter, the spring would not be so pleasant;
if we did not sometimes taste adversity, prosperity would
not be so welcome.

— *ANNE BRADSTREET*

The millions of us who want to chart a different course for
America must reclaim our power as citizens and overcome our
doubts and fears – as well as the bad habits that have lessened
our political effectiveness through the years.

— *DON HAZEN*

I must take issue with the term "a mere child," for it has been
my invariable experience that the company of a mere child is
infinitely preferable to that of a mere adult.

— *FRAN LEBOWITZ*

The person who is searching for his own happiness should pull
out the dart that he has stuck in himself – the arrowhead of
grieving, of desiring, of despair.

— *THE PALI TRIPITAKA*

All art is a challenge to despair.

— *E. C. BENTLEY*

The people in the marches were joyful, did you notice that?
Did you feel it yourself? The best smiles I've seen in years. Is
it not indeed joyful to embark on a life of great meaning?

— *DORIS HADDOCK*

I have to credit the Navy for rebuilding me, because when
I came to the Navy I didn't have any self-esteem or
feelings of worth.

— *ANTWONE FISHER*

JASON A. MERCHEY

I have been in Sorrow's kitchen and licked out all the pots.
Then I have stood on the peaky mountain wrapped in
rainbows, with a harp and a sword in my hands.
— ZORA NEALE HURSTON

There is looming up a dark new power... The enterprises of
the country are aggregating vast corporate combinations of
unexampled capital, boldly marking, not for economic
conquest only, but for political power. For the first time in our
politics, money is taking the field of organized power. The
question will arise, and arise in your day though perhaps not
fully in mine: "Which shall rule – wealth or man? Which shall
lead – money or intellect? Who shall fill public stations –
educated and patriotic free men, or the
feudal serfs of corporate wealth?"
— EDWARD RYAN

Every hour we invest on the job is an hour not invested directly
in our children, our mates, our community, our health,
our spiritual development, our search for meaning,
or our contribution to the larger life.
— VICKI ROBIN

Down, down, down into the darkness of the grave
Gently they go, the beautiful, the tender, the kind;
Quietly they go, the intelligent, the witty, the brave.
I know. But I do not approve. And I am not resigned.
— EDNA ST. VINCENT MILLAY

The grief of parting and the agony of separation are the ways of
the world.
— JAPANESE PROVERB

All sorrows can be borne if you put them into a story
or tell a story about them.
— ISAK DINESEN

THREE

What generates altruism is seeing oneself and others as human
beings of value, not being religiously faithful or adhering to
any particular theology.

— KRISTEN RENWICK MONROE

To many a refuge fear-stricken men betake themselves – to hills,
woods, groves, trees, and shrines. Nay, no such refuge is safe,
no such refuge is supreme. Not by resorting to such a refuge is
one freed from all ill.

— SIDDHARTHA GAUTAMA

Sometimes when you have everything,
you can't tell what really matters.

— CHRISTINA ONASSIS

The world revealed by modern science has been a world devoid
of spiritual purpose – opaque, ruled by chance and necessity,
and without intrinsic meaning. The human soul has not felt at
home in the modern cosmos – the soul can hold dear its music
and poetry, its private metaphysics and religion – but these find
no certain foundation in the empirical universe.

— RICHARD TARNAS

Whenever you get there, there's no "there" there.

— GERTRUDE STEIN

So many people walk around with a meaningless life. They
seem half-asleep, even when they're busy doing things they
think are important. This is because they're chasing the wrong
things. The way you get meaning in your life is to devote
yourself to loving others, devote yourself to your community
around you, and devote yourself to creating something that
gives you purpose and meaning.

— MORRIE SCHWARTZ

JASON A. MERCHEY

There's nothing more tragic than a young cynic because
then the person has gone from knowing nothing
to believing nothing.

— *MAYA ANGELOU*

O happiness, our being's end and aim,
Good pleasure, ease, content – whate'r thy name,
That something, still that prompts the eternal sigh:
For which we bear to live, or dare to die.

— *ALEXANDER POPE*

Adversity draws men together and produces beauty and
harmony in life's relationships, just as the cold of winter
produces ice-flowers on the window-panes, which vanish
with the warmth.

— *JEAN KERR*

[Spectator sports] occupies the population, and keeps them
from trying to get involved with things that really matter. In
fact, I presume that's part of the reason why spectator sports
are supported to the degree they are by dominant institutions.

— *NOAM CHOMSKY*

I'm doing what I think I was put on this earth to do. And I'm
really grateful to have something that I'm passionate about and
that I think is profoundly important.

— *MARIAN WRIGHT EDELMAN*

You are your choices.

— *JEAN PAUL SARTRE*

Live simply, and share time, energy, and material resources
with those who are in need.

— *THICH NHAT HANH*

THREE

To truly serve, purpose must be connected to our unique
authenticity. That is why money cannot serve as our purpose.
It can be a goal, but not a purpose.

— *LENEDRA J. CARROLL*

I know there is no other good in life but to be happy while one
lives. Indeed, every man who eats, drinks, and enjoys happiness
in his work – that is the gift of God.

— *ECCLESIASTES*

They say we all lose 21 grams at the exact moment of our
death. Everyone. How much fits into 21 grams?
How much is lost?

— *GUILLERMO ARRIAGA*

Within the child lies the fate of the future.

— *MARIA MONTESSORI*

We can flow along with the mainstream of a culture that does
not serve us well – does not really make us comfortable, does
not really make us safe; but only offers illusions of happiness,
comfort, safety – or we can begin the oftentimes prickly work
of searching our own hearts, of asking who and what we love,
who and what we feel strongly enough about to change our
lives for, to fight for, to live for.

— *DERRICK JENSEN*

You don't have to have a lot of hope, just keep working. When
we're involved in social change, the greatest thing is that we
meet people who teach how to live beyond hope.

— *FRAN PEAVEY*

On some level, punk [music] and Buddhism are underpinned
by a similar premise: Both acknowledge that the planet is
brimming with unhappiness. The question is how you
confront that misery.

— *A. C. THOMPSON*

JASON A. MERCHEY

May there be enough clouds in your life to make
a beautiful sunset.
— REBECCA GREGORY

The universe, which is not merely the stars and the moon
and the planets, flowers, grass and trees, but *other people*,
has evolved no terms for your existence, has made no room
for you, and if love will not swing wide the gates, no other
power will or can.
— JAMES BALDWIN

The continual pursuit of meanings – wider, clearer, more
negotiable, more articulate meanings – is philosophy.
— SUSANNE K. LANGER

Melancholy men are of all others the wittiest.
— ARISTOTLE

Unhurt people are not much good in the world.
— ENID STARKIE

I was hungry and you gave me meat; I was thirsty and you gave
me drink; I was a stranger and you took me in; I was naked and
you clothed me; I was sick and you visited me;
I was in prison and you came to me.
— JESUS OF NAZARETH

Quality of life does not have to do with income. Quality of life
has to do with having clean air, feeling safe in your house,
feeling that your children are safe in the streets, feeling that
you are valued as a human being, that you have good
relationships with other people, and that what you do
feeds your soul everyday.
— WINONA LADUKE

THREE

Life is a great surprise; I do not see why death should
not be an even greater one.

— *Vladimir Nabokov*

He who has a thousand friends has not a friend to spare.

— *Ali ibn Abu Talib*

When you take a stand, it shapes who you are. It sets your
priorities. It wakes you up in the morning, and it dresses you.
It puts you to bed at night. There's deep spirituality
in that way of being.

— *Lynne Twist*

Not every age is an age of heroes. In order for there to be such
larger-than-life figures among us, there must be great social
causes, such as just wars or liberation movements that call for
extraordinary leadership. Otherwise there are no heroic niches
to be filled, and we look elsewhere – to business, sports,
entertainment – for people to admire.

— *Robert W. Fuller*

Happiness is that state of consciousness which proceeds
from the achievement of one's values.

— *Ayn Rand*

One is happy as a result of one's own efforts, once one knows
the necessary ingredients of happiness – simple tastes, a certain
degree of courage, self denial to a point, love of work, and,
above all, a clear conscience. Happiness is no vague dream,
of that I now feel certain.

— *George Sand*

When it's dark enough, you can see the stars.

— *Charles A. Beard*

It takes patience to appreciate domestic bliss.
Volatile spirits prefer unhappiness.

— *George Santyana*

Here's your change. Paper or plastic? Credit or debit? You want
ketchup with that? I don't want a straw, I want real human
moments! I want to see you; I want you to see me.
I don't want to give that up, I don't want to be an ant.
— RICHARD LINKLATER

Gospel came from slavery. While pulling cotton they'd
moan…"Hmmm…" no one could stop them.
— MOSIE BURKS

There are, in fact, few stronger predictors of happiness than
a close, nurturing, equitable, intimate, lifelong companionship
with one's best friend.
— MARTIN E. P. SELIGMAN

The happiness of the drop is to die in the river.
— AL-GHAZALI

A nun told me when I was a freshman in college, "Make the
most of yourself, because you will never happen again."
That is the philosophy of my life.
— SHEILA LICHACZ

Let's create a world in which, when people see the Stars and
Stripes, they will think of us as the people who brought peace
to the world, who brought good-paying jobs to all its citizens
and clean water for the world to drink. In anticipation of that
day, I am putting my flag out today, with hope and with pride.
— MICHAEL MOORE

The orgasm has replaced the cross as the focus of longing and
the image of fulfillment.
— MALCOLM MUGGERIDGE

"Meaning" is typically spoken about by those at universities, but everyone engages in the search for meaning every day. Just as it suggests, the term gets at the ideas, "What does something *mean*?" and "What is the significance of this?" For example, questions such as, "Why do we (humans) exist?" "Why do bad things happen to good people?" and "Why should I get out of bed today?" are definitely questions about meaning. Existentialism, a philosophical movement born in the earlier part of the 20th century, re-questions things that humankind, over the course of many centuries, confidently tried to explain. It is about "creating meaning;" in other words, establishing the answers to questions that face us here on Earth, today. Believers in God feel that they understand the answers to some of life's important questions, but I feel that the individual can take a more difficult but more solid path: to think independently about what human life is for and how we can make the most of it. Noted thinker Irving Singer etched this quotation in the marble floor of the eternal temple of the wise: "A life of mere self-preservation, for which we may well have instincts, would be for most of us a life without meaning. We want something beyond the routine of a boring and aimless existence." This is the essence of humanism: we have the privilege and responsibility to consider deep questions and to courageously bear the answers and the difficulty in finding solid answers. In doing so, one can aspire to one's chosen values, and hopefully find fulfillment in the process.

HUMOR, LIGHT-HEARTEDNESS, & ACCEPTANCE OF THE ABSURD

My colleagues don't call me the "Wise Guy" for nothing. This chapter is a lot of laughs, both entertaining and enlightening. You will find dry, clever, and absurd quotations from all types of folks, addressing a colorful range of subtopics within the values of humor, light-heartedness, and "acceptance of the absurd." Absurdity is plainly apparent when we're open to seeing it, and perhaps, for better mental health, attempting to accept it or resist it! True to the jester within, I quote those who poke fun at the power mongers in government, who satirize big business, and who lay bare organized religion. No offense intended, I just think it's important to make light of the heavier issues that face us today. Whereas most teenage boys tried to figure out how to party without getting caught, I spent a lot of my time making video satires. Sometimes the videos were politically incorrect, sometimes incisive, and usually full of nonsense. Lightheartedness can soften the hard lines that divide us and provide tolerance during challenging times. It is in those raw, uncensored moments when laughter takes our breath away that we can see things anew and, ideally, glimpse ways to improve our society.

He deserves paradise who makes his companions laugh.

— *THE KORAN* 53

JASON A. MERCHEY

There is one way to find out if a man is honest – ask him.
If he says "yes," you know he is crooked.
— *GROUCHO MARX*

What makes this country strong is not economic might. No.
What makes it strong is that all these beautiful, wonderful
cultures live here. And what are we doing? Heading into
the twenty-first century with English only.
— *EDWARD JAMES OLMOS*

Men seem to kick friendship around like a football,
but it doesn't seem to crack. Women treat it as glass
and it goes to pieces.
— *ANNE MORROW LINDBERGH*

"Money isn't everything," according to those who have it.
— *MALCOLM S. FORBES*

Any woman who thinks the way to a man's heart is through
his stomach is aiming about 10 inches too high.
— *ADRIENNE E. GUSOFF*

See them floundering after their cherished possessions,
like fish flopping in a river of starved water.
— *SIDDHARTHA GAUTAMA*

If Bush has his way, the Iraqis will be enjoying their universal
health care system just as Medicaid gets savaged at home. They
will be counting up their personal oil profits while Americans
face deep cuts in Temporary Assistance to Needy Families, the
Earned Income Tax Credit, food stamps, and education at all
levels. They will be free to practice democracy in its untidiest
forms, while Americans can be spied on and incarcerated
without charges under Patriot Acts I and II.
— *BARBARA EHRENREICH*

FOUR

We demand freedom of speech and freedom of the
press…although we have nothing to say and nothing
worth printing.

— KAHLIL GIBRAN

Apparently you can't be friends anymore with somebody
who is of a different [political] party.

— JOHN MCCAIN

Analyzing humor is like dissecting a frog. Few people
are interested and the frog dies of it.

— E. B. WHITE

History is cruel, for it forces on us the immediate and urgent
problem that seems to require immediate action and answers.
Old answers are used and are invariably
disappointing in results.

— MARCUS G. RASKIN

Don't worry. Be happy.

— MEHER BABA

Let me tell you something that we Israelis have against Moses.
He took us 40 years through the desert in order to bring us
to the one spot in the Middle East that has no oil!

— GOLDA MEIR

Is it not strange that desire should so many years
outlive performance?

— WILLIAM SHAKESPEARE

When you know to laugh and when to look upon things as too
absurd to take seriously, the other person is ashamed to carry
through even if he was serious about it.

— ELEANOR ROOSEVELT

What you really value is what you miss, not what you have.
— *JORGE LUIS BORGES*

An optimist is a man who gets treed by a lion,
but enjoys the scenery.
— *WALTER WINCHELL*

Man is trampled by the same forces he has created.
— *JUANA FRANCES*

Things are not as they seem. Nor are they otherwise.
— *THE LANKAVATARA SUTRA*

Good taste and humor are a contradiction in terms,
like a chaste whore.
— *MALCOLM MUGGERIDGE*

Life is worth being lived, but not being discussed all the time.
— *ISABEL ADJANI*

Whether exploring the depths of the human soul or the depths
of matter, artists and mystics and scientists have come
face-to-face with chaos and disorder. But the opened mind
thrives on difference and remains open to the contradictory.
— *F. BARRON, A. MONTUORI, & A. BARRON*

Our soldiers are being killed in Iraq; Osama's still on the loose;
jobs are being exported all over the world; the deficit has
reached biblical proportions. And our president is
worrying about Mars and marriage?
— *MAUREEN DOWD*

CHAPTER FOUR

Only when the last tree has died, and the last river has been poisoned, and the last fish have been caught, will we realize we cannot eat money.

— CREE INDIAN SAYING

Thirty-five is when you finally get your head together and your body starts falling apart.

— CARYN LESCHEN

We were taught that we were good people, religious people, the chosen people, but we didn't think we were chosen to die [in the Holocaust]. I was just a little kid. I did nothing wrong to anybody: I went to school, I had good grades, and I minded my mother and father. I could not think of a reason why I should be murdered.

— HAROLD GORDON

We faced an impossible choice between bankruptcy, breaking the law, or forgoing my father's lifesaving treatments.

— JULIA WHITTY

I was rather disappointed that fellow clergymen would see my nonviolent efforts as those of an extremist.

— MARTIN LUTHER KING, JR.

The only way to save America is to root out the humanist from all walks of life.

— HOMER DUNCAN

I think it's terribly arrogant and overly ambitious for this President to think he can invade that country, turn it into a democracy, and use American taxpayer dollars to build an infrastructure that still is not built in some parts of this nation.

— MAXINE WATERS

JASON A. MERCHEY

I was thrown out of college for cheating on the metaphysics
exam; I looked into the soul of the boy sitting next to me.
— *WOODY ALLEN*

Reality is a crutch for people who can't cope with drugs.
— *LILY TOMLIN*

I have learned silence from the talkative, toleration from the
intolerant, and kindness from the unkind; yet strange,
I am ungrateful to these teachers.
— *KAHLIL GIBRAN*

Alas, I am dying beyond my means.
— *OSCAR WILDE*

They say that God is everywhere, and yet we always think
of Him as somewhat of a recluse.
— *EMILY DICKINSON*

Fanatics are those people who know that they are doing what
God would be doing if he only had all the facts.
— *GEORGE SANTYANA*

I realize I've been tempted by the thought of respectability,
seduced by credibility…and you know what? Screw everybody
if they don't respect me. I make people laugh.
— *JIM CARREY*

We didn't do anything wrong. That's the important thing. We
live in a weird world. This country will forgive you rape, will
forgive you murder, will forgive you anything but success.
— *KATHIE LEE GIFFORD*

Oh, to be seventy again!
— *OLIVER WENDELL HOLMES*

CHAPTER FOUR

Health is a crown, and no one knows it save a sick person.
— *Swahili proverb*

There are no persons capable of stooping so low as those
who desire to rise in the world.
— *Marguerite Blessington*

A pessimist is one who feels bad when he feels good for fear
he'll feel worse when he feels better.
— *Author Unknown*

Life is happier if it is full of pretty people.
— *Jilly Cooper*

Many persons are both wise and handsome – but they would
probably be still wiser were they less handsome.
— *The Talmud*

Nothing in the affairs of men is worthy of great anxiety.
— *Plato*

Earth laughs at him who calls a place his own.
— *Hindustani proverb*

It ain't those parts of the Bible that I can't understand that
bother me; it is the parts that I do understand.
— *Mark Twain*

In America, sex is an obsession.
In other parts of the world, sex is a fact.
— *Marlene Dietrich*

If thine enemy wrong thee, buy each of his children a drum.
— *Chinese proverb*

JASON A. MERCHEY

What should the reasonable woman make of this world?
If God is omniscient, omnipresent, omnipotent, and benevolent,
Why does his creation – wondrous human beings,
Face atrocity wrought by nature unbridled
and humans malevolent?

— *Jason Merchey*

For a list of all the ways technology has failed to improve
the quality of life, please press three.

— *Alice Kahn*

The only thing that can stop a teenage boy is a teenage girl.

— *Robert Transpota*

God will provide – if only God would provide until he provides.

— *Hanan J. Ayalti*

I'll not listen to reason...
Reason always means what someone else has to say.

— *Elizabeth Gaskell*

When did Christmas shopping become a patriotic duty, the
contemporary equivalent of collecting tin cans in World War II?

— *Katha Pollitt*

Sin is a dangerous toy in the hands of the virtuous. It should
be left to the congenitally sinful, who know when to play with
it and when to let it alone.

— *H. L. Mencken*

It is easier to rule a kingdom than to regulate a family.

— *Japanese proverb*

Satire should, like a polished razor keen,
Wound with a touch that's scarcely felt or seen.
— *MARY WORTLEY MONTAGU*

Another reason America's great is because we create things
here, things of unique beauty. Things that unconsciously
interweave the American attributes of ingenuity, optimism,
gluttony and narrow-mindedness. Things like "All You Can Eat"
restaurants, the Clapper, street legal semi-automatic grenade
weapons, the temporary insanity plea, cutting-edge CD-ROM
technology used for porn, deep fried cheese, bans on toy guns,
rain ponchos for dogs, Orange Julius, Orange County, beer can
hats, plea bargaining, and being able to plug your parents
with bullets and get acquitted.
— *DENNIS MILLER*

Stoop and you'll be stepped on; stand tall and you'll be shot at.
— *CARLOS A. URBIZO*

You seek for knowledge and wisdom as I once did; and I
ardently hope that the gratification of your wishes may not
be a serpent to sting you as mine has been.
— *MARY SHELLEY*

Why is it that our memory is good enough to retain the least
triviality that happens to us, and yet not good enough to
recollect how often we have told it to the same person?
— *FRANCOIS, DUC DE LA ROCHEFOUCAULD*

Women are never stronger than when they arm themselves
with their weakness.
— *MARIE DE VICHY-CHAMROND*

JASON A. MERCHEY

Many of the insights of the saint stem from his
experience as a sinner.
— *ERIC HOFFER*

On my good days I'm agnostic; on my bad days I'm an atheist.
— *SHOLEH IRAVANTCHI*

Insane people are always sure they're just fine. It's only the sane
people who are willing to admit they're crazy.
— *NORA EPHRON*

Women have a special talent for understanding men
better than he understands himself.
— *VICTOR HUGO*

We should live and learn; but by the time we've learned,
it's too late to live.
— *CAROLYN WELLS*

Small children disturb your sleep; big children, your life.
— *YIDDISH PROVERB*

If one's ambitions are overdemanding, one is aware of only
the negative side of life, and even of oneself.
— *ANITA VÉLEZ-MITCHELL*

The Kremlin is no more Communistic than the
Vatican is Christian.
— *LEONARD LEEMAN*

I love the freedom [of stand-up comedy]. I love the art of it
and the power of it; to use humor and make people think.
— *PAUL RODRÍGUEZ*

FOUR

…many younger Americans get their news from Jon Stewart or "Saturday Night Live." And why not, when one of the greatest financial beneficiaries of the war in Iraq seems to be a corporation once led by the vice president? You couldn't make this stuff up.

— ANNA QUINDLEN

People come to Las Vegas for the opportunity to do better for their families. But you can't have sex and drugs and gambling and expect to raise a healthy family. Look around.

— LINDA SKIPP

The knowledge that something remains yet unenjoyed impairs our enjoyment of the good before us.

— SAMUEL JOHNSON

I survived many times in my life by learning to laugh at myself.

— ANTONIA NOVELLO

It's just a job; grass grows, birds fly, waves pound the sand – I beat people up.

— MUHAMMAD ALI

Life is pleasant. Death is peaceful.
It's the transition that's troublesome.

— ISAAC ASIMOV

The secret of eternal youth is arrested development.

— ALICE R. LONGWORTH

The first half of our lives is ruined by our parents
and the second half by our children.

— CLARENCE DARROW

JASON A. MERCHEY

The government is concerned about the population
explosion, and the population is concerned about
the government explosion.

— *RUTH RANKIN*

If God lived on earth, all his windows would be broken.

— *YIDDISH PROVERB*

If my theory of relativity is proven successful, Germany will
claim me as a German... Should my theory prove untrue,
Germany will declare that I am a Jew.

— *ALBERT EINSTEIN*

Aren't women prudes if they don't, and prostitutes if they do?

— *KATE MILLER*

I acted alone on God's orders and I have no regrets.

— *YIGAL AMIR*

We are all born charming, fresh, and spontaneous – and must
be civilized before we are fit to participate in society.

— *JUDITH MARTIN*

It's a sad reality that so many of our heralded peacemakers
were wretches at home. Gandhi was vindictive to his wife and
sons, as was Tolstoy. Martin Luther King, Jr. was a pathetic
husband. Einstein was emotionally cruel to his wives. Yet, look
at Harry Truman. He idolized his wife and was the model
family man. Then he dropped the bombs on Hiroshima and
Nagasaki, and killed tens of thousands of families.

— *COLMAN MCCARTHY*

I see God in every human being. When I wash the leper's
wounds, I feel I am nursing the Lord himself.

— *MOTHER TERESA*

FOUR

Having chicks around is the kind of thing that breaks up the
intense training. It gives you relief, and then afterward you go
back to the serious stuff.

— ARNOLD SCHWARZENEGGER

In the name of Hippocrates, doctors have invented the most
exquisite form of torture ever known to man: survival.

— LUÍS BUÑUEL

Adults are always asking kids what they want to be when they
grow up 'cause they're trying to get ideas.

— PAULA POUNDSTONE

America's moral ills were defined in the '80s and '90s in terms
that reflected the traditional conservative worries, with a focus
on things like crime, drugs, premarital sex, and divorce. Other
concerns – little problems like greed, envy, materialism, and
inequality – have been excluded from the values debate.

— DAVID CALLAHAN

We could now reproduce our 1948 standard of living
(measured in marketed goods and services) in less than half
the time it took in 1948. We actually could have chosen the
four hour day. Or a working year of six months.

— JULIET SCHOR

The fates dealt Al Gore and the United States a weird hand
in 2000. He got the most votes but the other guy became
president. And the country, its Treasury looted and its most
pressing needs deliberately ignored, has been rolling
backward ever since.

— BOB HERBERT

What's that you say? You want to talk to a real human being in
"customer service?" HA HA HA! Press "4" and kiss the rest
of your day goodbye.

— MICHAEL MOORE

Parenthood: that state of being better chaperoned
than you were before marriage.

— MARCELENE COX

Can we imagine a world where Hindus and Muslims are not
killing each other in India and Pakistan and Kashmir? A world
where Jerry Falwell and company are not calling hell and
damnation down onto others made in the image of God?

— MATTHEW FOX

The thief, on the point of breaking into a house,
calls on God for help.

— HEBREW PROVERB

If you live long enough, you'll see that every victory
turns into a defeat.

— SIMONE DE BEAUVOIR

We spend our time searching for security
and hate it when we get it.

— JOHN STEINBECK

Sometimes you just have to bow to the absurd.

— MELINDA M. SNODGRASS

My sense of humor has always been quite unique. I have known it
to be a strength, a liability, a compulsion, and a mechanism to bring
about a change – be it in mood or between myself and others. I get a
legal high from being witty and pushing the bounds of typical
conversation. My mother, who really wanted a sweet, conforming child,

FOUR

was ambivalent at first about my inquisitive and outgoing side, which was reflected in my interest in telling jokes, interacting with adults, and saying what was on my mind. This lifelong pursuit of the funny, the light, and recognizing the absurd became the foundation for my including these values in this book, for I do indeed think all three are worthy of praise and integral to one's happiness. When I do not have a connection with a stranger, humor opens things up like an ocean breeze. When I am uncomfortable, a little foolhardiness or sarcasm seems to lighten the mood. I derive joy from and often feel camaraderie with others in humor. And there is so much absurdity out there in the universe – perhaps especially in the American corner of the universe – that to recognize it and attempt to accept it or rail against it seems to me to be part of living wisely. But most of all, humor seems to tap into the silly, mischievous, and wry side of me – the part that wants to make a mockery out of both the precious and the incredulous: "Since the house is on fire, let us warm ourselves" ~ Italian proverb.

CREATIVITY, INGENUITY, & VISION

I don't think you often find "vision" alongside the typical virtues, such as truth, beauty, and wisdom. Yet it has a unique property that the wise are aware of, and I think, is worthy of pursuit and cultivation. Vision encompasses an inner knowing, a visualization of what is possible for us and our world, and a willingness to see what is not readily apparent to the naked eye (or the naked mind!). Ingenuity is highly regarded though, particularly in America. As a young country, we constantly rely upon the ingenuity of Americans to help this country grow and to establish her as a key player in the global marketplace. But we will need a heaping dose of ingenuity to extricate ourselves and the rest of the world from the waist-deep problems that plague our society. Creativity is something more than painting or sculpting or composing a beautiful song; it is the development of alternatives and solutions to humanity's most urgent and most pressing issues. "Thinking outside the box" and "looking with new eyes" are metaphors for the divergent thinking that is creativity. Viewing and living life creatively can help put our world back on track so that we may all achieve the greatest things possible. If we can invent a nuclear bomb, what is stopping us from eliminating poverty?

I never took hallucinogenic drugs because I never wanted my consciousness expanded one unnecessary iota.

— *FRAN LEBOWITZ*

JASON A. MERCHEY

Smart ideas are a dime a dozen, unless you can figure out all
the thousands of little details that give life to an idea so
that the idea can survive.

— VICTOR VILLASEÑOR

To a mind that is still the whole universe surrenders.

— CHUANG TZU

Even the most farseeing, the most humane are also men of
their times and consequently cannot be expected to transcend
them too often without being marginalized.

— MARCUS G. RASKIN

When I am alone the flowers are really seen;
I can pay attention to them. They are felt presences.

— MAY SARTON

How many of us recognize our enormous debt
to Gene Roddenberry?

— JOHN A. MARSHALL

If there is a storm on the horizon of our life, how can we learn
to see the signs in our sleep walking state before it is too late?
How do we listen to the still voice within?
Where are the guides we can trust?

— WILLIAM CUMMINGS

Faith is the bird that feels the light and sings when
the dawn is still dark.

— RABINDRANATH TAGORE

My favorite thing is to go where I have never been.

— DIANE ARBUS

CHAPTER FIVE

The human mind is a miracle. Once it accepts a new idea
or learns a new fact, it stretches forever and never goes back
to its original dimension. It is limitless. No one has even
guessed its potential.

— LEO BUSCAGLIA

Though there is a movement to recover creativity and spirit
within the corporate organizational structure, this is still
an embryonic movement.

— JUSTINE WILLIS TOMS & MICHAEL TOMS

No matter what anybody tells you, words and ideas
can change the world.

— THOMAS SCHULMAN

You can't use up creativity. The more you use,
the more you have.

— MAYA ANGELOU

I know of no more encouraging fact than the unquestionable
ability of man to elevate his life by a conscious endeavor.

— HENRY DAVID THOREAU

Don't limit your child to your own learning, for he was
born in another time.

— RABBINICAL SAYING

In Chinese, the word for crisis is wei ji, composed of the
character wei, which means danger, and ji, which means
opportunity.

— JAN WONG

There is nothing sacred in the temple, in the mosque,
in the churches. They are all the inventions of thought.

— JIDDU KRISHNAMURTI

JASON A. MERCHEY

Clearly, the Western mode of consciousness produces certain
ideas and not others. When the qualities of information
conveyed through empathy, intuition, and the consciousness
that created Stonehenge cannot even be properly
communicated, they simply cease to exist.
And not surprisingly, powers of imagination once
so active in childhood fall into disuse.

— *HELEN PALMER*

The eager and often inconsiderate appeals of reformers and
revolutionists are indispensable to counterbalance the inertia
and fossilism marking so large a part of human institutions.

— *WALT WHITMAN*

Everyone has a talent; what is rare is the courage to follow the
talent to the dark place where it leads.

— *ERICA JONG*

If they give you ruled paper, write the other way.

— *JUAN RAMON JIMINEZ*

America must finish what we started in the Declaration of
Independence and the Constitution and go all the way until we
assure liberty and justice for the millions of children of all races
and incomes left behind in our society today despite national
leaders who seek to turn us back to the not-so-good old days
of race and class and gender divisions.

— *MARIAN WRIGHT EDELMAN*

Like Einstein's theories, Spinoza's greatest work, Ethics,
expressed its rational mysticism behind logical abstractions
while concluding that nature's harmony proves God's
existence, and that elegant simplicity – the "oneness" that
Einstein had long hoped to find in the elusive unified field
theory – holds the key to all understanding.

— *THOMAS J. MCFARLANE*

You can muffle the drum, and you can loosen the strings of the
lyre, but who can command the skylark not to sing?

— *KAHLIL GIBRAN*

Why accept darkness over seeing,
When the light can actually be lit?
The funny thing about smog being,
That over time, you fail to notice it.

— *JASON MERCHEY*

Love thy neighbour as yourself,
but choose your neighbourhood.

— *LOUISE BEAL*

Such as men themselves are, such will God himself
seem to them to be.

— *JOHN SMITH*

Maybe in another life and time I would have been king.

— *ANTWONE FISHER*

[Plato's ideal society] guarantees to all people the right to an
education that diagnoses and perfects their unique talents, plus
a work role that conveys a sense of self-esteem, saving them
from the neuroses of megalomania and the lust for power. It
forbids privilege and sexism and all other criteria irrelevant to
merit. It eliminates conflict of interest from those who hold
office and gives the masses a potent checklist they can use to
hold their rulers to account. Best of all, it eliminates all traces
of "might makes right" and serves as a pattern laid up in
heaven to rank actual societies in terms of what corrupts them.
Society becomes more corrupt as the struggle
for power becomes more brutal...

— *JAMES R. FLYNN*

JASON A. MERCHEY

Anyone who says you can't see a thought simply
doesn't know art.
— *Wynetka Ann Reynolds*

When I am...completely myself, entirely alone...or during the
night when I cannot sleep, it is on such occasions that my ideas
flow best and most abundantly. Whence and how these come
I know not, nor can I force them.
— *Wolfgang Amadeus Mozart*

People see God every day; they just don't recognize him.
— *Pearl Bailey*

It is better to build bridges than walls.
— *Swahili proverb*

The only thing that can save this world is the reclaiming
of the awareness of the world. That's what poetry does.
— *Allen Ginsburg*

Reason is man's primary tool for survival.
— *Ayn Rand*

We live in a wonderful world that is full of beauty, charm and
adventure. There is no end to the adventures we can have
if only we seek them with our eyes open.
— *Jawaharlal Nehru*

Dance alone and you can jump all you wish.
— *Greek proverb*

The creative process is one of surrender, not control.
— *Julia Cameron*

The more we realize our minuteness and our impotence in the
face of cosmic forces, the more astonishing becomes what
human beings have achieved.

— BERTRAND RUSSELL

If you believe everything you read, better not read.

— JAPANESE PROVERB

Simple dry atheism, although descriptive of my beliefs about
the literal existence of gods and spirits, was not sufficient to
express my developing world view; I didn't just *disbelieve*
something, I also began to *believe* in something: in living life
fully, awarely, and in the here and now, instead of shutting
myself off from it out of some misguided notion that such
alienation is "spiritual." I began to find myself saying things
like, "The truly spiritual path does not lead us out of the world
but through the midst of the world," and, "This life, this world,
is holy." For me, calling the universe "god" does not accurately
convey my experience of it. Rather than making the universe
my god, I prefer to view my experience as one of having gone
beyond the god-oriented paradigm, from "having a god" to
embracing something more elemental and profound: Life
Itself, the Cosmos Itself, as an ever-changing tapestry in which
I am one thread contributing to the living pattern.

— KARYN MILOS

The world's leaders are full of pious hypocrisy, and they need to
be exposed and replaced. But many of the people I know are
beginning to ask a different set of questions. Not which power
tools do we use to destroy a system, but which surgical
instruments will help us create better alternatives.

— EBOO PATEL

The philosopher inspires the scientist to search
for verifiable knowledge.

— LEONARD LEEMAN

JASON A. MERCHEY

If I spent enough time with the tiniest creature – even a
caterpillar – I would never have to prepare a sermon.
So full of God is every creature.
— *Meister Eckhart*

If I had influence with the good fairy who is supposed to
preside over the christening of all children, I should ask that
her gift to each child in the world be a sense of wonder so
indestructible that it would last throughout life.
— *Rachel Carson*

The capacity to transcend the situation is an inseparable part of
self-awareness, for it is obvious that the mere awareness of one's
self as a being in the world implies the capacity to stand outside
and look at one's self and the situation and to assess and guide
one's self by an infinite variety of possibilities.
— *Rollo May*

Making mental connections is our most critical learning tool –
the essence of human intelligence: to forge links; to go beyond
the given; to see patterns, relationship, context.
— *Marilyn Ferguson*

Things don't change. You change your way of looking, that's all.
— *Carlos Castaneda*

I had nothing to offer anybody except my own confusion.
— *Jack Kerouac*

The new religion will teach the dignity of human nature and its
infinite possibilities for development. It will teach the solidarity
of the race and that all must rise and fall as one. Its creed will
be justice, liberty, equality for all the children of earth.
— *Elizabeth Cady Stanton*

FIVE

Almost any description of the creative experience…gives
experiential accounts which are in important respects
analogous with those obtained from people at play.

— MIHALY CSIKSZENTMIHALYI

Every discovery contains an "irrational element"
or creative intuition.

— KARL POPPER

Without leaps of imagination, or dreaming, we lose the
excitement of possibilities. Dreaming, after all,
is a form of planning.

— GLORIA STEINEM

Many people see things but few understand them.

— YIDDISH PROVERB

Surrealism is the most exhilarating adventure of the mind, an
unparalleled means of pursuing the fervent quest for freedom
and true life beyond the veil of ideological appearances. Only
the social revolution…will enable the true life of poetry and
mad love to cast aside, definitively, the fetters of degradation
and dishonor, and to flourish with unrestrained splendor.

— FRANKLIN ROSEMONT

What was once Sinclair Lewis is buried in no ground. Even in
life he was fully alive only in his writing. He lives in public
libraries from Maine to California, in worn copies on the
bookshelves of women from small towns who, in their girlhood,
imagined themselves as Carol Kennicotts, and of medical men
who, as youths, were inspired by Martin Arrowsmith.

— DOROTHY THOMPSON

JASON A. MERCHEY

Intelligence recognizes what *happened*.
Genius recognizes what *will happen*.

— JOHN CIARDI

My mother wanted us to live through our third eyes, to see life
as possibility. She wanted us to imagine a world free of
patriarchy, a world where gender and sexual relations could be
reconstructed. She wanted us to see the poetic and prophetic
in the richness of our daily lives. She wanted us to visualize
a more expansive, fluid, "cosmos-politan" definition of
blackness, to teach us that we are not merely inheritors
of a culture but its makers.

— ROBIN D. G. KELLEY

It may be that religion is dead, and if it is, we had better know
it and set ourselves to try to discover other sources of moral
strength before it is too late.

— PEARL S. BUCK

Whatever in the past has been the moral justification for
violence – whether defense against attack, or the overthrow of
tyranny – must now be accomplished by other means. It is the
monumental moral and tactical challenge of our time. It will
make the greatest demands on our ingenuity, our courage,
our patience, and our willingness to renounce old habits –
but it must be done.

— HOWARD ZINN

Wandering gives me a new set of eyes – or removes adulthood's
blinders from the ones I have. It is permission to see as well as
to wander, to be an archaeologist of my own life.

— CATHY JOHNSON

No heart has ever suffered when it goes in search of its dreams.

— PAULO COEHLO

Look into the future and consider the consequences. Think
about the real advantages to yourself, then wonder about the
impact on others and how that might reflect back on your life.
Imagine how you might righteously defend your position.

— BENJAMIN FRANKLIN

[America has] incredibly difficult issues and an honest search
for solutions can only come from a sustained effort by the
broadest array of America's brightest and wisest men
and women. What the U.S. really needs is leadership that
could marshal that effort.

— BOB HERBERT

Where would we be without prophets, visionaries,
nonconformists, ironists, and dissenters? The great ethical
traditions, both religious and secular, as well as literature and
the arts, are filled with eccentrics – complex characters who
challenge, inspire, and irritate those around them. They flaunt
conventional wisdom, stubbornly champion new and unsettling
ideals, love those whom others deem unlovable, or are
themselves considered strange and unlovable.

— ELIZABETH KISS

The perfumed flowers are our sisters;
The deer, the horse the great eagle, these are our brothers.
The rocky crests, the juices of the meadows, the body heat of
the pony, and man –
All belong to the same family.

— CHIEF SEATTLE

The cinema has no boundaries; it is a ribbon of dreams.

— ORSON WELLS

Creative minds have always been known to survive
any kind of bad training.

— ANNA FREUD

JASON A. MERCHEY

When two do the same thing, it is not the same thing after all.
— PUBLILIUS SYRUS

The world of learning is so broad, and the human soul is so
limited in power! We reach forth and strain every nerve, but we
seize only a bit of the curtain that hides the infinite from us.
— MARIA MITCHELL

Nonviolent direct action seeks to create such a crisis and foster
such a tension that a community which has consistently refused
to negotiate is forced to confront the issue. It seeks to
dramatize the issue so that it can no longer be ignored.
— MARTIN LUTHER KING, JR.

Many times when I stop working on a problem consciously, my
mind continues to work on it below the surface. Often
solutions come to me quite by surprise. I've learned over time
to allow that to happen, rather than to feel that I can simply
solve the problem by continuous grueling effort.
— MARILYNNE ROBINSON

The artist is simply the medium between his fantasies
and the rest of the world.
— FEDERICO FELLINI

Masterpieces are not single and solitary births; they are the
outcome of many years of thinking in common, of thinking
by the body of the people, so that the experience of the mass
is behind the single voice.
— VIRGINIA WOOLF

Now that the United States and the rest of humanity have
begun to confront the natural limits to our resources, we are in
need of a new vision – a vision of a sustainable economy.
— HERMAN E. DALY

FIVE

Even when I was very little I read volumes and volumes of
books. I also loved to write because writing allowed my
imagination to take me anywhere. It was a form
of expression and escape.

— *DIANA L. VARGAS*

The goal of Don Juan Matus' shamanism is to break the
parameters of historical and daily perception and to perceive
the unknown. That's why he called himself a navigator of
humanity. He asserted that infinity lies beyond the perimeters
of daily perception. To break these parameters was the
aim of his life.

— *CARLOS CASTANEDA*

America stands at the peak of a world historical arc that marks
globalization's tipping point from a closed club of the
privileged few to a planetwide reality.
Making that strategic vision – that happy ending –
come true will end war as we know it.

— *THOMAS P. M. BARNETT*

I'm nobody's steady date. I can always be distracted by love,
but eventually I get horny for my creativity.

— *GILDA RADNER*

An idea is a greater monument than a cathedral.

— *CLARENCE DARROW*

I have the feeling that I don't write my books, that the story is
somewhere floating. My job is to be quiet, to be silent and
alone, and ready to tune in to those voices and write the story.

— *ISABEL ALLENDE*

A wise man will make more opportunities than he finds.

— *FRANCIS BACON*

JASON A. MERCHEY

The creative adult is the child who has survived.

— *URSULA K. LEGUIN*

We see that the apparent contradictions and perplexities in
every religion mark but different stages of growth. The end
of all religions is the realizing of God in the soul.
That is the one universal religion.

— *SRI SWAMI VIVEKANANDA*

To create is to make something whole from the pieces of our
lives and, in the process, to become more whole ourselves,
seeing with more clarity each of those pieces, understanding
where they fit, how they matter. It is a healing act, a leave-taking
from the chaos as one moves from the choppy surface toward
the stillness of the center.

— *JAN PHILLIPS*

If we knew the extent to which Indian ideas have shaped
American culture, the United States might recognize Native
American societies as cultural assets from which we could
continue to learn.

— *JAMES W. LOEWEN*

It is hard to let old beliefs go. They are familiar. We are
comfortable with them and have spent years building systems
and developing habits that depend on them. Like a man who
has worn eyeglasses so long that he forgets he has them on, we
forget that the world looks to us the way it does because we
have become used to seeing it that way through a particular
set of lenses. Today, however, we need new lenses.

— *KENICH OHMAE*

...Being too full of sleep to understand
How far the unknown transcends the what we know.

— *HENRY WADSWORTH LONGFELLOW*

Look at everything as if you were seeing it for the first or last
time. Then your time on earth will be filled with glory.

— BETTY SMITH

Life without logic would be no better than groping in the dark.
Rationality can illumine our paths. But we must grasp our
ultimate goals with a perception greater than what the
mind alone can offer.

— TOM MORRIS

Reason has a legitimate function to fulfill, for which it is
perfectly adapted; and this is to justify and illumine for man his
various experiences and to give him faith and conviction in
holding on to the enlarging of his consciousness. But reason
cannot arrive at any final truth because it can neither get
to the root of things nor embrace their totality.

— SRI AUROBINDO

The problem with the rat race is that even if you win,
you're still a rat.

— LILY TOMLIN

Art, to a certain extent and at a given moment, is a force which
blows the roof off the cave where we are imprisoned.

— ERNEST HELLO

A child's world is fresh and new and beautiful, full of wonder
and excitement. It is our misfortune that for most of us,
that clear-eyed vision, that true instinct for what is beautiful
and awe-inspiring is dimmed and even lost before
we reach adulthood.

— RACHEL CARSON

The law of possibility catches my brain on fire; the winner
of a race is the winner before the race began.

— JOHN A. MARSHALL

JASON A. MERCHEY

Poetry is what makes the invisible appear.
— *NATHALIE SARRAUTE*

God is not the voice in the whirlwind; God is the whirlwind.
— *MARGARET ATWOOD*

Is it a mere coincidence that the Chinese suffix "tse,"
which has come to mean "master," literally means "child?"
— *BENJAMIN HOTH*

Out of each experience, enough light is generated to
illuminate another little stretch. Who knows where it will lead?
— *CESAR CHAVEZ*

History, a nightmare from which I am trying to awake.
— *JAMES JOYCE*

Benjamin Franklin snatched lightning from the sky
and the scepter from tyrants.
— *ANNE ROBERT JACQUES TURGOT*

Thought is a universe of freedom.
— *JEWISH PROVERB*

About 3,650 B.C., an Emperor of China, Hwang Ti, noted
that "all the blood in the body is under the control of the
heart...the blood flows continuously in a circle and never
stops." More than 4,000 years were to pass before experimental
data – William Harvey's in 1916 – supported the theory
that the heart functions as a pump.
— *ISAAC ASIMOV*

Keep your eyes on the stars and your feet on the ground.
— *THEODORE ROOSEVELT*

We ourselves feel that what we are doing is just a drop in the
ocean; I think the ocean would be less because of that missing
drop. I do not agree with the big way of doing things.

— MOTHER TERESA

What we are today comes from our thoughts of yesterday, and
our present thoughts build our life of tomorrow. Our life is a
creation of our mind.

— THE PALI TRIPITAKA

About that transcendent feeling we get when we have an idea,
when we work productively, when we create, Mihaly Csikszentmihalyi
claims: "'Flow' denotes the holistic sensation present when we act with
total involvement. It is the kind of feeling after which one nostalgically
says, 'That was fun' or 'That was enjoyable.'" Artists agree that time seems
to disappear when they are involved in their craft, as do scientists
pursuing a discovery and explorers entering a new territory. The
divergence, passion, and spontaneity that characterize ingenuity is
absolutely fascinating. It is also the impulse that seems to account for how
humans got from there (prehistoric) to here (post-industrial). Ingenuity
simply generates movement toward a creation; the term does not make a
value judgment about the goodness or badness inherent in the discovery.
Manipulation of nuclear fission, for example, is neither inherently right
nor wrong (hence the nearly limitless capacity of the nucleus to provide
humans with electric power, while being able to destroy cities in seconds).
Creativity and ingenuity are also remarkable because they are our keys to
the chaotic room in which we humans have locked ourselves; problems
such as overpopulation, global warming, and the savage inequity of
resource distribution will require nothing less than a dynamic plan to free
us in this millennium.

DEDICATION, RESPONSIBILITY, & WILL

I often imagine what the world would be like if everyone was living at his or her highest potential. Perhaps it is simpleminded to think that the world would be incredibly different, but doing so leads us to a more potent question: What would *your* life look like if *you* were living at *your* highest potential? It's easy to complain about the world around us, or others in relationship to us, but I believe we far too often underestimate what is possible in the world *within* us. Think of a time when you have observed someone at the height of his or her game – an Olympic athlete, a celebrated musician, or a powerful speaker. What you observed was the by-product of practice, dedication, and will applied to a chosen endeavor over a long period of time. Look inside yourself and envision the great life that you have the potential to live, for as George Eliot said, "It is never too late to be what you might have been."

One of the biggest reasons politicians continue to trample on issues of crucial importance to low-income Americans – issues like jobs, education, and access to health care – is the traditionally poor voting habits of that segment of the population.

— BOB HERBERT

JASON A. MERCHEY

I have lost friends, some by death...
others by sheer inability to cross the street.

— VIRGINIA WOOLF

The easy route is not always the right route.

— JOHN J. GEORGE

If I can do anything to make sure that not just my daughter but
every child in America has green pastures to run in and clean
air to breathe and clean water to swim in, then that is
something I'm going to work my hardest to make happen.

— BARACK OBAMA

9/11 was actually the catalyst for outrages that I was feeling for
a long time. I said to myself, "It's time for women to make a
statement against war and all the other madness –
we have to speak out."

— JENNI PRISK

Even the dead hand of the past, as in outmoded customs or
bureaucracies, retains its power over the present only by
a constantly renewed acquiescence among those who
submit to it.

— IRVING SINGER

My grandfather worked three jobs to buy property so that they
could have a place to live and educate all five of his children.
These are people who took charge of their lives. I can't believe
that life is more complicated today than it was for them.

— CONDOLEEZZA RICE

You must see [the struggle in Iraq] through, and I believe that
you will. It is related to the larger struggle. You must put in
place moderates who can create a modern society. If you walk
away from Iraq, jihadis will follow you wherever you go.

— LEE KUAN YEW

My address is like my shoes; it travels with me.
I abide where there is a fight against wrong.

— *MARY JONES*

We will have no national security until we are willing to invest
in the health, skills, and character of our children. And this
cannot be done on the cheap.

— *PAUL WELLSTONE*

Complacency is the enemy. We cannot really learn anything
until we rid ourselves of complacency. Our attitude towards
ourselves should be "insatiable in learning" and towards others
to be "tireless in teaching."

— *MAO ZEDONG*

If you can't feed a hundred people, then feed just one.

— *MOTHER TERESA*

There are solutions that will see us through to a safer, more
ecologically and socially harmonious future. The challenge is
primarily political. The dominant forces and leaders in our
society, along with many average citizens, are resisting the
necessary changes, for a myriad of reasons.

— *BETSY TAYLOR*

Moderate effort over a long time is important, no matter what
you are trying to do. One brings failure upon oneself by
working extremely hard at the beginning, attempting to do
too much, and then giving it all up after a short time.

— *TENZIN GYATSO*

Want to make something of yourself?
Then to go to school and work your ass off.

— *DAVID CALLAHAN*

JASON A. MERCHEY

When you put your hand to the plow, you can't put it down
until you get to the end of the row.

— *ALICE PAUL*

Fashion is something barbarous, for it produces innovation
without reason and imitation without benefit.

— *GEORGE SANTYANA*

Authority and place demonstrate and try the tempers of men
by moving every passion and discovering every frailty.

— *PLUTARCH*

We all know what character is, not because we can define it
exactly, but because we know when we have seen it. We know
when we have exercised character; at those times we feel clean.

— *MARIANNE WILLIAMSON*

The way to do fieldwork is
never to come up for air until it is all over.

— *MARGARET MEAD*

Do not fear when your enemies criticize you –
beware when they applaud.

— *VO DONG GIANG*

Thoughts held in mind reproduce after their kind. It's the
nature of thinking. What we hold in our mind reproduces
itself in the reality of our life and our experience.

— *MARY MANIN MORRISSEY*

We can believe what we choose; we are answerable
for what we choose to believe.

— *JOHN HENRY NEWMAN*

CHAPTER SIX

The mad mind does not halt. If it halts, it is enlightenment.
— *Zen proverb*

The enduring value of the relationship to the land might best
be measured by the extent to which it evolves beyond self-
interest. All healthy relationships entail sacrifice and are never
solely about what makes one person feel good, but are about
what's also good for someone else. Relationship implies a
responsibility that goes beyond one's own dreams.
— *Peter Forbes*

Many Americans draw the boundaries of their self-interest
very narrowly. Our culture's emphasis on individualism and
competition reinforces an attitude of isolation
and impotence toward global problems.
— *Betsy Taylor*

In terms of spoiling the environment and using world
resources, we are the world's most irresponsible
and dangerous citizens.
— *Donella H. Meadows*

One may not be able to direct the course of one's life,
but one is responsible for trying to.
— *John A. Marshall*

It is not enough to be compassionate, you must act.
— *Tenzin Gyatso*

When we "agree to disagree," we are agreeing
to perpetuate the problem.
— *John Konstanturos*

JASON A. MERCHEY

We have too many people who do what they're told; it's
plantation politics. Patriotism demands debate. That means
questioning authority in the tradition of the civil rights
movement and the Vietnam War.

— *Tavis Smiley*

Oh yeah, life goes on,
Long after the thrill of living is gone.

— *John Mellencamp*

My father said, "There are times to sit,
or stand and be counted,"
When good people die, just laws are forsaken,
banned books smolder.
There comes a time when our steed must be
armored and mounted;
The balance of good and evil rests on our collective shoulders.

— *Jason Merchey*

Many nations have seen their fortunes fall, not because they
didn't understand what was wrong, but because they didn't
have the will to correct it; the citizenry became cynical.

— *Patricia Schroeder*

Making justices justify and presidents preside in a spirit of
openness and accountability – that's what gives us moral clarity
when we need it.

— *Jonathan Alter*

Organizing and disciplining our mental processes clears
away the clamor and allows us to hear the inner voices of our
body's needs and knowledge.

— *Lenedra J. Carroll*

CHAPTER SIX

Sacrifice is bitter, but its fruits are sweet.

— *PHILIPPINE PROVERB*

Effort is only effort when it begins to hurt.

— *JOSÉ ORTEGA Y GASSET*

One, I take responsibility. Two, I make no apologies.
Three, I stuck to my oath.

— *GLORIA M. ARROYO*

I've learned to ignore my moods.

— *CHRISTOPHER REEVE*

It is noble to fight wickedness and wrong; the mistake
is in supposing that spiritual evil can be overcome by
physical means.

— *LYDIA MARIA CHILD*

In the long run, every man will pay the penalty for his own
misdeeds. The man who remembers this will be angry with no
one, indignant with no one, revile no one, blame no one,
offend no one, hate no one.

— *EPICTETUS*

The last decades have shown us that ordinary people can
bring down institutions and change policies that seemed
entrenched forever.

— *HOWARD ZINN*

Universal responsibility is the real key to human survival. It is
the best foundation for world peace, the equitable use of
natural resources, and through concern for future generations,
the proper care of the environment.

— *TENZIN GYATSO*

I don't wait for moods. You accomplish nothing if you do that.
Your mind must know it has got to get down to work.
— PEARL S. BUCK

The war for total brotherhood must be a nonviolent war
carried on by methods worthy of the ideals we seek to serve.
The acts we perform must be the responsible acts of free men,
not the irresponsible acts of conscripts under orders. We must
fight against institutions but not against people.
— DAVE DELLINGER

Whoever falls and gets up gains a step.
— HEBREW PROVERB

Industry is a better horse to ride than genius.
— WALTER LIPPMAN

At the start of any big climb I feel afraid, I dread the discomfort
and danger that I shall have to undergo. It's like standing on
the edge of a cold swimming pool trying to nerve yourself to
take the plunge; yet once in, it's not nearly as bad as you
feared; in fact, it's enjoyable... Once I start climbing,
all my misgivings are forgotten.
— CHRIS BONINGTON

People fighting for justice in this country and around the world
have every reason to be discouraged, but in fact there are signs
of hope that we should be aware of. Anyone familiar with my
work in Congress knows that I don't give up easily.
If anything, I've just gotten started.
— NYDIA M. VELÁZQUEZ

I don't see how something like a confession and a few
repetitions of the "Hail Mary" are going to solve any problems.
— GIAMPAOLO SERVADIO

Said the Holy One to Israel, "I have told you that when you
pray you should do so in the synagogue in your city. If you
cannot pray in the synagogue, pray in your field. If you cannot
pray in your field, pray in your house. If you cannot pray in
your house, pray on your bed. If you cannot pray on your bed,
meditate in your heart."

— *MIDRASH PSALMS 4:9*

We were all shocked when we realized the extent to which the
chimpanzees across Africa were disappearing. The time had
come for me to use the knowledge I had acquired to try
to help the chimps in their time of need.

— *JANE GOODALL*

Where luck is wanting, diligence is useless.

— *SPANISH PROVERB*

I am very patient – despite what my mother says.

— *NATASCHA WHIPPLE*

Skeptical of theories of redemption, damnation, and
reincarnation, secular humanists attempt to approach the
human situation in realistic terms: human beings are
responsible for their own destinies.

— *PAUL KURTZ*

It has been my observation that being beaten is often a
temporary condition; giving up is what makes it permanent.

— *MARILYN VOS SAVANT*

As of 2003, there are over ninety United Nations resolutions
that are being violated by countries around the world.

— *JASON MERCHEY*

JASON A. MERCHEY

For unto whomsoever much is given,
of him shall be much more required...
— LUKE 12:48

When you're dancing with a bear,
you can't stop dancing until the bear gets tired.
— JOYCELYN ELDERS

Our goal is not to *be* happy, our goal is to bring happiness
to others. That is the only way *to be* happy.
— JORDAN S. METZGER

Many persons have a wrong idea of what constitutes true
happiness. It is not attained through self-gratification but
through fidelity to a worthy purpose.
— HELEN KELLER

The greatest purveyor of violence in the world today
is my own government.
— MARTIN LUTHER KING, JR.

We flatter those we scarcely know,
We please the fleeting guest,
And deal full many a thoughtless blow
To those we love the best...
— ELLA WHEELER WILCOX

With malice toward none, with charity for all, with firmness in
the right as God gives us to see the right,
let us finish the work we are in.
— ABRAHAM LINCOLN

For many years, and through the reports of many wars, I have
frequently wondered what we are doing to the human race,
and to our beautiful planet, as we ravage land and peoples.
Mothers' sons are killing mothers' sons.
— JENNI PRISK

Duty is lighter than a feather, but heavier than a mountain.

— *MEIJI TENNO*

In the confrontation between the stream and the rock, the stream always wins – not through strength but perseverance.

— *ANONYMOUS*

Lots of people want to ride with you in the limo, but what you want is someone who will take the bus with you when the limo breaks down.

— *OPRAH WINFREY*

Liberals don't hate America. We love America more than Ann Coulter does. I love it enough to engage my readers honestly.

— *AL FRANKEN*

We have to stay there as long as it takes and take care of it once and for all. No one wants another September 11.

— *JESSICA PORTER*

Friendship is always a sweet responsibility, never an opportunity.

— *KAHLIL GIBRAN*

If you've done well in your profession, your obligation is to spend about half your time sending the elevator back down – to help others fulfill themselves.

— *KEVIN SPACEY*

It's not funny, or cute, that I stayed on the road as long as I did [driving at eighty-eight with macular degeneration]. Nor did I beat the system. I'm just an old person who should have known better. Luck was with me and I got away with it. What if I had an accident, hurt someone, or worse? There is no way I could have found any peace or joy in living the rest of my life after that.

— *RUTH G. NEDBOR*

JASON A. MERCHEY

Slow and steady wins the race.

— *AESOP*

[America], if you proceed much further down the slippery
slope, people around the world will stop admiring the good
things about you. They'll decide that your city upon the hill is a
slum and your democracy is a sham, and therefore you have no
business trying to impose your sullied vision on them.
They'll think you've abandoned the rule of law.
They'll think you've fouled your own nest.
The British used to have a myth about King Arthur. He wasn't
dead, but sleeping in a cave, it was said; in the country's hour
of greatest peril, he would return. You, too, have great spirits of
the past you may call upon: men and women of courage, of
conscience, of prescience. Summon them now, to stand with
you, to inspire you, to defend the best in you. You need them.

— *MARGARET ATWOOD*

Your children need your presence more than your presents.

— *JESSE JACKSON*

Volunteering is at the very core of being a human. No one has
made it through life without someone else's help.

— *HEATHER FRENCH*

My dad was a man who loved whiskey and women and fighting.
With my childhood, it's a wonder I'm not psychotic. I was a
little Jewish boy in the non-Jewish neighborhood. It was a little
like being the first Negro enrolled in the all-white school.
I was isolated and unhappy. I grew up in libraries and among
books, without friends.

— *ABRAHAM MASLOW*

I've tried to get beyond polarization.

— *MURRAY BOWEN*

One reason for my hope lies in the tremendous energy,
enthusiasm, and commitment of a growing number of young
people around the world. As they find out about the
environmental and social problems that are now part of their
heritage, they want to fight to right the wrongs.

— *Jane Goodall*

George W. Bush is not the problem. Nor is the high-spending
Congress that oils the war machine. I'm the problem. I need to
figure out how to be a better husband, a better father,
a better writer, a better teacher.

— *Colman McCarthy*

I take very seriously trying to live in a manner that I believe in.

— *Katherine Melcher*

From one point of view, personal liberation without freeing
others is selfish and unfair, because all sentient beings also have
the natural right and desire to be free of suffering.

— *Tenzin Gyatso*

The greatest responsibility an individual assumes is to oneself.

— *Madeline Bartosch*

Bullies use the word "patriotism" to shoot down virtually all
criticism of the current conservative geopolitical agenda, sort of
a missile-defense system against original thought, open debate,
and the free exchange of ideas. And to my mind, this abuse of
language is an affront to any real patriot, who knows that
public discussion and informed debate is at the root of what
once made America (and to a certain extent Britain, too) great.
It is the dissenters who are the true patriots.

— *Anita Roddick*

JASON A. MERCHEY

The greatest happiness you can have is knowing that you do
not necessarily require happiness.

— WILLIAM SAROYAN

In our every deliberation, we must consider the impact of our
decisions on the next seven generations.

— GREAT LAW OF THE IROQUOIS

The tender word forgotten,
The letter you did not write,
The flower you might have sent,
Are your haunting ghosts tonight.

— MARGARET E. SANGSTER

Self-restraint may be alien to the human temperament,
but humanity without restraint will dig its own grave.

— MARYA MANNES

Laws are partly formed for the sake of good men, in order to
instruct them how they may live on friendly terms with one
another, and partly for the sake of those who refuse to be
instructed, whose spirit cannot be subdued, or softened, or
hindered from plunging into evil.

— PLATO

When you have your own children you will understand your
obligation to your parents.

— JAPANESE PROVERB

For a hundred that can bear adversity, there is hardly one
that can bear prosperity.

— THOMAS CARLYLE

Sometimes the best helping hand you can get
is a good firm push.

— *Joan Thomas*

The world has achieved brilliance without wisdom, power
without conscience. Ours is a world of nuclear giants and
ethical infants.

— *Omar Bradley*

Every day undertake something that is difficult for you and try
to do it. Though you fail 5 times, keep on, and as soon as you
have succeeded in that direction, apply your concentrated will
on something else. You will thus be able to accomplish
increasingly greater things. Will is the instrument of the
image of God within you.

— *Paramahansa Yogananda*

Love provides the motive, the energy for discipline. It is the will
to extend oneself for the purpose of nurturing one's own,
or another's, spiritual growth.

— *M. Scott Peck*

The easiest way for your children to learn about money
is for you not to have any.

— *Katharine Whitehorn*

A good case can be made for the proposition that, although
involved or passionate commitment to some cause or ideal is
normally healthy and happiness-producing, devout, pious, or
fanatic commitment to the same kind of cause or ideal is
potentially pernicious and frequently (though not always)
does much more harm than good.

— *Albert Ellis*

JASON A. MERCHEY

Every man is the son of his own works.
— *Miguel de Cervantes*

I need my conscience to keep watch over me
To protect me from myself,
So I can wear honesty like a crown on my head
When I walk into the promised land.
We've been too long American dreaming
And I think we've all lost the way.
— *Brendan Perry & Lisa Gerrard*

Here is a test to find whether your mission on earth is finished:
If you're alive, it isn't.
— *Richard Bach*

An element of abstention, of restraint, must enter
into all the finer joys.
— *Vida D. Scudder*

Whatever a man soweth, that shall he also reap.
— *Paul 6:7*

It is our responsibility to carry on the spirit, bravery, and
patriotism of our nation's fallen heroes of 9/11/2001.
The world has witnessed our country's strength in a time
of great sorrow. Let us use that strength to create a better
world for all its people.
— *Carolyn La Pierre*

I never blame failures – there are too many complicated
situations in life, but I am absolutely merciless
toward lack of effort.
— *F. Scott Fitzgerald*

Dedication is a value that I have had much experience with, yet understand little of. Sure, I studied very hard in college; I've been in love relationships and longed to leave; I exercise regularly. However, I have never had to face the ceaseless flow of days upon days in a POW camp. Or the rigors of running a marathon. I have not felt the conflicting emotions of wanting to sleep through my child's crying in the next room. As much weight as I can lift, there are other, heavier barbells to move up to. The will that is required to make decisions, to confront one's own mortality, or to deal with anxiety is similar to the discipline that is required to run our country. I am writing of a mindset in which one pushes one's self to impose structure, to "stay the course," to continue even after one yearns for rest. During the years I spent reading books and compiling quotations for VALUES OF THE WISE, I tried to find the dedication and discipline to increase my understanding of the lofty virtues I was studying. There were so many silent nights, the only sound being that of my typing. And though it may have felt like labor, it was a labor of love: "Duty does not have to be dull. Love can make it beautiful and fill it with life" ~ Thomas Merton.

CHAPTER SEVEN

HONOR, INTEGRITY, & MORALITY

Honor is a concept that I think is misunderstood and does not get the respect it so rightly deserves. It is more than just following orders, fighting well, or having a good family reputation. To me, and many of those included in the following pages, honor is one of the core components to a *life of value*. It is about looking within and deciding what the right thing to do is *and then doing it.* In other words, morality is the brain deciding what is right and wrong, and honor is the will and strength to carry it out. Oftentimes honor is associated with aggression and militarism, but it need not be so limited. It is just as much about admitting one made a mistake or letting a person back in line after he asked you to hold his place. And honor is behaving in ways that are consistent with your values. Honor is a lofty word that sets a high standard, for what a world we would live in if more societal leaders and protectors such as politicians, police, military, and corporate decision-makers acted honorably; racism, war, pettiness, and corruption would go the way of slavery!

It's a matter of taking the side of the weak against the strong,
something the best people have always done.

— HARRIET BEECHER STOWE

JASON A. MERCHEY

Philosophy, like morality itself, is first and last an exercise in reason – the ideas that should come out on top are the ones that have the best reasons on their sides.

— JAMES RACHELS

A person, no matter his nationality, is a human being. After I saw her being slapped twice, I slipped into her hospital room and told her "Don't worry." Then I walked six miles to the nearest Marines and told them where she was.

— MOHAMMED AL-REHAIEF

We cannot hope to scale great moral heights by ignoring petty obligations.

— AGNES REPPLIER

Money often costs too much.

— RALPH WALDO EMERSON

To appear rich, we make ourselves poor.

— MARGUERITE BLESSINGTON

Character is power.

— BOOKER T. WASHINGTON

There is one lesson I have learned that I hold above all others from my experience as a father, teacher, community organizer, and U.S. senator: We should never separate the lives we live from the words we speak. To me, the most important goal is to live a life consistent with the values I hold dear and to act on what I believe in.

— PAUL WELLSTONE

Part of being a champ is acting like a champ. You have to learn how to win and not run away when you lose.

— NANCY KERRIGAN

SEVEN

A child, a drunkard and a fool tell the truth.

— *HUNGARIAN PROVERB*

Sure it is possible to argue for a world trade system that puts
basic human rights and the environment at its core. It's
possible but it's damned hard when you have the most
powerful corporations in the world raging against you.

— *ANITA RODDICK*

This inconsistency is such, as you too shall adore,
I could not love you dear so much, loved I not honor more.

— *RICHARD LOVELACE*

As you go to fight this dubious war in Iraq, Jesús, my son, I want
to tell you so many things that fill my head and heart. I want
you to remember, above all, the moral values you inherited
from your Hispanic roots, and the respect for others. Always
remember that you are not an assassin; be disciplined, don't
abuse the enemy, but don't be a coward either. Be firm, but not
merciless; don't take advantage of a person who is weak, even if
he is the enemy. Be a humanitarian: always help your fallen
companions, and help the injured no matter what side they are
on. Wear your American soldier's uniform with pride, but wear
with even greater pride your heritage of an Aztec warrior. No
matter what happens, you will always have here, in this small
corner of the world, your father, your mother, and family. Son,
take good care of yourself, be brave and strong of spirit so we
will have the fortune of having you return to us, without
honors, without medals, but alive.

— *FERNANDO SUÁREZ DEL SOLAR*

Morality is its own advocate; it is never necessary
to apologize for it.

— *EDITH L. HARRELL*

JASON A. MERCHEY

Bringing about a more just and humane society – indeed, world – is not just a matter of comfort; research shows a connection between social position and health. Literally, the society we humans have set up and perpetuate brings about not only the suffering of some people, it can exact an incalculable cost – untimely death.

— *JASON MERCHEY*

We do not celebrate the death of our enemies.

— *YITZHAK RABIN*

The essence of immorality is the tendency to make an exception of myself.

— *JANE ADDAMS*

Henceforth, the only honorable course will be to stake everything on a formidable gamble: that words are more powerful than munitions.

— *ALBERT CAMUS*

While living I want to live well. I know I have to die someday, but even if the heavens were to fall on me, I want to do what is right.

— *GERONIMO*

The character issue has become a central part of recent presidential campaigns, but it has always focused on sexual license. There are more important things.

— *ANNA QUINDLEN*

I hope I shall always possess firmness and virtue enough to maintain what I consider the most enviable of all titles: Honest Man.

— *GEORGE WASHINGTON*

SEVEN

When you come from a place of truth, and if you align yourself
with that which is right, and true, and good – that which you
know will serve to help other people –
then nothing can stop you.

— *BRENDA REED*

Like a beautiful flower, full of color but without scent, are the
fair but fruitless words of him who does not act accordingly.

— *DHAMMAPALA*

The most exhausting thing in the world is being insincere.

— *ANNE MORROW LINDBERGH*

Can such a petty pleasure as slave-produced sugar compensate
for so much misery produced among our fellow creatures, and
such a constant butchery of the human species by this
pestilential, detestable traffic in the bodies of souls of men?

— *BENJAMIN FRANKLIN*

It's naive to expect partisan politicians to play fair, I know; still,
I'm always surprised by the boldness of their hypocrisies.

— *WENDY KAMINER*

"I love ya, bro, you know that, so I gotta tell you a little secret
we white people have: Your people aren't ever going to have it
as good as we do. And if you think that working hard and
trying to fit in is going to get you a seat on the board of
directors when we've already got our black seat filled – well,
friend, if it's equality and advancement you seek, try Sweden."
The sooner we start talking like that, the more honest a society
we'll all be living in.

— *MICHAEL MOORE*

Better to lose your eye than your good name.

— *ARMENIAN PROVERB*

JASON A. MERCHEY

Of course no one wants to say the world would be better off with Saddam Hussein's sadistic and brutal regime in place, but that isn't the question on the table. The issue is whether or not the end justifies the means. Yes, removing Saddam Hussein is ultimately a good thing. But if deceit and manipulated information are what got us to this point, we must cry out against it. We have no guarantee of being "better off" the next time our government uses such tactics.

— *Julia Reid*

Christopher Columbus told his Spanish patrons, the king and queen, that the pagan Indians he had met readily embraced Christianity…"they are always smiling…their speech is the sweetest and gentlest in the world…they are a loving people, without covetousness…weapons they have none…it appears that the people are ingenuous and would be good servants."

— *Isaac Asimov*

I am not leaving. You do not have the power to release me, least of all to release me to gratify yourselves. I shall not leave this place until I hear that everybody else has been released, and that all the laws of the tyranny have been stricken from the books.

— *Nelson Mandela*

I do everything for a reason.
Most of the time the reason is money.

— *Ava Gardner*

I know there are some good white people, but the soldiers must be mean to shoot children and women. Indian soldiers would not do that to white children.

— *Louise Weasel Bear*

SEVEN

Men are disposed to live honestly, if the means of doing
so are open to them.

— THOMAS JEFFERSON

You have heard the sound of the white soldier's axe upon the
little pines. His presence here is an insult to the spirits of our
ancestors. Are we then to give up their sacred graves to be
ploughed for corn? Dakotas, I am for war.

— RED CLOUD

Man holds in his mortal hands the power to abolish all forms of
human poverty, and all forms of human life. And yet the same
revolutionary beliefs for which our forbearers fought
are still at issue around the globe.

— JOHN F. KENNEDY

Because duties are context-bound, the particular circumstances
and possible consequences will affect which moral duties are
most important in any given situation.

— JUDITH A. BOSS

How we...deal with the present crisis in our church
will do much to define us as Catholics.

— SEAN O'MALLY

You can stand tall without standing on someone.
You can be a victor without having victims.

— HARRIET WOODS

Most women have it [a power over men], but once you start to
abuse it – once you start to manipulate people with it – you
become lame. It's no longer a power but a fault. The secret to
using power is not to use it. Just having it is enough.

— JESSICA ALBA

JASON A. MERCHEY

A warrior deems life a light thing when compared to honor.
— *JAPANESE PROVERB*

We have allowed our institutions to be taken over in the name
of a globalized American empire that is totally alien
in concept to anything our founders had in mind.
— *GORE VIDAL*

If the society today allows wrongs to go unchallenged, the
impression is created that those wrongs have the approval
of the majority.
— *BARBARA JORDAN*

I am poor and my only inheritance is my honor.
— *RAFAEL CHACÓN*

It is the extreme willingness of adults to go to almost any length
on the command of an authority…
— *STANLEY MILGRAM*

Altruists have a particular perspective in which all mankind is
connected through a common humanity, in which each
individual is linked to all others and to a world in which all
living beings are entitled to a certain humane treatment
merely by virtue of being alive.
— *KRISTEN RENWICK MONROE*

If the will be set on virtue, there will be no
practice of wickedness.
— *CONFUCIUS*

Action indeed is the sole medium of expression for ethics.
— *JANE ADDAMS*

SEVEN

We should feel humiliated that some of our intellectuals,
supposedly the representatives of our nations' consciences and
the defenders of their liberty and dignity, not only dealt with
Saddam Hussein, but also supported him…
The Arabs should have been the ones to bring down Saddam,
in defense of their own dignity and their own true interests.

— OSAMA AL-GHAZALI HARB

Lying is an accursed vice. It is only our words which bind us
together and make us human.

— MICHEL DE MONTAIGNE

There is no man more dangerous, in a position of power, than
he who refuses to accept as a working truth the idea that all a
man does should make for rightness and soundness, that even
the fixing of a tariff rate must be moral.

— IDA M. TARBELL

There is some good in this world, and it's worth fighting for.

—J. R. R. TOLKIEN

Wal-Mart is the largest corporation in the world. Wal-Mart
makes its prices low by exploiting its own workers;
they average $15,000 a year with puny health care benefits.

— JIM HIGHTOWER

I never ran my train off the track, and I never lost a passenger.

— HARRIET TUBMAN

On my medal, the Yad Vashem medal, there is an inscription. It
says, "Whoever saves one life, he has saved the entire
humanity." And I think the inversion of that is also true:
whoever kills one innocent human being,
it is as if he has killed the entire world.

— OTTO, RESCUER OF JEWS DURING WWII

JASON A. MERCHEY

It is the spirit of trade unionism that is most important, the
service of fellowship, the feeling that the hurt of one is the
concern of all and that the work of the individual benefits all.
— *ROSE SCHNEIDERMAN*

Honesty of manhood and womanhood will abolish the sources
of discontent which threaten the world's civilization, and will
bring us to conviction regarding the fundamentals
of the social fabric, without which fundamentals there
can be no human progress.
— *WARREN G. HARDING*

For me, the chimpanzees [with their impending extinction]
must always come first... I am in a position, thanks to being
able to work with such wonderful creatures, to be able to reach
out a hand towards them. If I fail to do that, for any reason
whatsoever, it would be a betrayal of all that I have learned
during my years of working with them.
— *JANE GOODALL*

Reproach yourself ten times when you reproach others once.
— *VIETNAMESE PROVERB*

Religion, blushing, veils her sacred fires,
And unaware, as morality expires.
— *ALEXANDER POPE*

War is not merely justifiable, but imperative, upon honorable
men, upon an honorable nation, where peace can only be
obtained by the sacrifice of conscientious conviction
or of national welfare.
— *THEODORE ROOSEVELT*

What would Jesus say about Enron?
— *JOHN LELAND*

SEVEN

The United States of America is still run by its citizens. The
government works for us. Rank imperialism and warmongering
are not American traditions or values. We do not need to
dominate the world. We want and need to work with other
nations. We want to find solutions other than killing people.
Not in our name, not with our money,
not with our children's blood.
— MOLLY IVINS

For 3,500 years, Jews have been telling themselves, their
children, and the rest of the world: Be good. Be kind.
Be honest. Be ethical. Be moral. It is the most
revolutionary message in human history...
— JEFF JACOBY

It's a shame and a sin that we've got political leaders here in
the United States who are eliminating jobs at the same time
that they're telling people to get to work.
— MARIAN WRIGHT EDELMAN

Propriety governs the superior man; law, the inferior man.
— CHINESE PROVERB

While the message of excess materialism is toxic for all our
children, it is especially cruel for the one out of six American
children living in poverty. I often wonder how sporting goods
executives sleep at night after marketing basketball shoes to
low-income children that cost a minimum-wage-earning
parent nearly a week's salary to pay for.
— NYDIA M. VELÁZQUEZ

Young men acting contrary to the good of their community
have not yet learned the real essence of maleness.
— RUDOLFO A. ANAYA

JASON A. MERCHEY

Much of the social progress of the past two centuries can be credited to the courage and energy of the pioneers who introduced reforms such as public health, the abolition of slavery, and even democracy itself, often against the violent oppression of the established order. Such progress would scarcely have been possible without the belief that one's conscience should be one's guide.

— ROY BROWN

The silk worker may make beautiful things, fine shimmering silk. When it is hung up in the window of Altman's or Macy's or Wanamaker's it looks beautiful. But the silk worker never gets a chance to use a single yard of it. And the producing of the beautiful thing, instead of being a pleasure, is instead a constant aggravation to the silk worker. They make a beautiful thing in the shop and then they come home to poverty, misery, and hardship. They wear a cotton dress while they are weaving the beautiful silk for some demi monde in New York to wear.

— ELIZABETH GURLEY FLYNN

You were given the choice between war and dishonor.
You chose dishonor and you will have war.

— WINSTON CHURCHILL

It is essential that we find that balance between materialism and morality.

— ARUN GANDHI

When morality comes up against profit,
it is seldom profit that loses.

— SHIRLEY CHISHOLM

When profits and performance are the only measure of success,
old-fashioned ideas about fairness go out the window.

— DAVID CALLAHAN

SEVEN CHAPTER

When rulers lead lives of luxury, they tend to forget human suffering. Accordingly when they used the word "sacrifice," it smells of hypocrisy.

— SEHUI CHO

Weapons of mass destruction would be a noble lie because you're convinced that this war is the right thing to do and you are the wise few, the elite, who are leading the stupid masses, and the stupid masses aren't going to agree to sacrifice their lives for nothing – for the glory of the nation – unless their own survival is at stake.

— SHADIA DRURY

The conscientious moral agent is someone who is concerned impartially with the interests of everyone affected by what he or she does; who carefully sifts facts and examines their implications; who accepts principles of conduct only after scrutinizing them to make sure they are sound; who is willing to "listen to reason" even when it means that earlier convictions may have to be revised; and who, finally, is willing to act on the results of this deliberation.

— JAMES RACHELS

Honor is self-esteem made visible in action.

— AYN RAND

History will not be kind to the chicanery that passes for governing in the Bush II administration.

— BOB HERBERT

Saddam Hussein had chemical weapons in the 1980s, and it didn't make any difference to U.S. policy. Shaking hands with dictators today can turn them into Saddams tomorrow.

— TOM BLANTON

JASON A. MERCHEY

Moral theories can be compared to road maps.
A good theory offers guidance or signposts for thinking
about and resolving moral issues.
— *JUDITH A. BOSS*

What we committed in the Indies stands out among the most
unpardonable offenses ever committed against God and
mankind, and this trade in Indian slaves is one of the most
unjust, evil, and cruel among them.
— *BARTOLOMÉ DE LAS CASAS*

I shall die, but that is all that I shall do for Death;
I am not on his pay-roll.
— *EDNA ST. VINCENT MILLAY*

Though the ethical challenges we face in the workplace may be
different from those in our personal lives, the principles of
ethical conduct that apply to those challenges do not change.
There is no such thing as business ethics – there is only ethics.
— *MICHAEL S. JOSEPHSON*

The world has never yet seen a truly great and virtuous nation,
because in the degradation of women, the very fountains of life
are poisoned at their source.
— *LUCRETIA MOTT*

Then I, however, showed again by action, not in word only, that
I did not care a whit for death, but that I did care with all my
might not to do anything unjust or unholy.
— *SOCRATES*

Escaping with your reputation is better than
escaping with your property.
— *HAUSA PROVERB*

SEVEN

William J. Bennett, author of *The Book of Virtues* and one of the nation's most relentless moral crusaders, is a high-rolling gambler who has lost more than $8 million at casinos in the last decade. Pressed, he said, "My gambling days are over."

— KATHERINE Q. SEELYE

What the people want is very simple.
They want an America as good as its promise.

— BARBARA JORDAN

The need for an eternal moral order is one of the deepest needs of our breast.

— WILLIAM JAMES

The privacy of public men can be measured by a kind of algebra of exposure: the prominence of their position multiplied by the variance between their espoused beliefs and their actual behavior; what might be called the hypocrisy quotient.

— ANNA QUINDLEN

When the rich wage war, it's the poor who die.

— JEAN-PAUL SARTRE

The only thing that doesn't abide by majority rule is a person's conscience.

— HARPER LEE

If you're a person of integrity, the question ends there. And if you're not a person of integrity, all the appearances in the world don't give you integrity. So I prefer substantive integrity [to] apparent integrity.

— RAVI BATRA

JASON A. MERCHEY

I'm really glad that our young people missed the Depression,
and missed the great big war. But I do regret that they missed
the leaders that I knew. Leaders who told us when things were
tough, and that we would have to sacrifice, and these
difficulties might last awhile.

— ANN RICHARDS

Moral thought seems to behave like all other kinds of thought.
Progress through the moral levels and stages is characterized
by increasing differentiation and increasing integration,
and hence is the same kind of progress that
scientific theory represents.

— LAWRENCE KOHLBERG

We can't leave people in abject poverty, so we need to raise the
standard of living for eighty percent of the world's people,
while bringing it down considerably for the twenty percent
who are destroying our natural resources.

— JANE GOODALL

The Master said, "The gentleman understands what is moral.
The small man understands what is profitable."

— CONFUCIUS

...unethical behavior both stems from and reinforces
destructive mental factors such as greed and anger. Conversely,
ethical behavior undermines these and cultivates mental factors
such as kindness, compassion, and calm. Ultimately, after
transpersonal maturation occurs, ethical behavior is said to flow
spontaneously as a natural expression of identification with all
people and all life.

— FRANCES VAUGHAN & ROGER WALSH

Since when do you have to agree with people
to defend them from injustice?

— LILLIAN HELLMAN

SEVEN

If we are to wage a campaign against these Indians, the
proposed end should be their extermination, or their removal
beyond the lakes of the Illinois river. The same world
will scarcely do for them and us.

— *THOMAS JEFFERSON*

If our honor as a nation is to be restored, it is not by letting
the mighty shield themselves by bringing the law to bear
against their pawns. It is by bringing the law to bear
against the mighty themselves.

— *AL GORE*

I combined honor, integrity, and morality in the same chapter
because these *values of the wise* are related to one another in clear and
significant ways. Honor was the first value I began to research in 2001,
when I began compiling evidence for the present values as being *the
values that wise persons aspire to and seek to cultivate within themselves.*
One of the striking elements to this set of virtues is the fact that there is a
lot of self-sacrifice involved in being honorable, having integrity, and
trying to be moral. Often, there is no direct reward, but a kind of cost –
as when you turn in a found wallet to the police station – with the
hundred dollar bill still inside. I believe that the noble persons
throughout history who thought about and tried to aspire to honor
gleaned a type of satisfaction by "taking the high road." I imagine they
were intrinsically rewarded – even if those around them didn't appreciate
the depth of their self-monitoring – for, as John Naber put it: "It's the
tough decisions that really test our character, for character is revealed
when the price of doing the right thing is more than we want to pay."

CHAPTER EIGHT

LIBERTY & PEACE

Liberty has been one of humanity's greatest ideas and concerns since the dawn of civilization. Our country finds renewed appreciation for the liberty she was founded on, especially given the current state of political unrest in many parts of the world. After all, as Thomas Jefferson knew, without liberty one can't have a "full" life or pursue happiness. Nor can one experience the peace that he envisioned and that we have longed for. I have explored many noteworthy statements on liberty and find it interesting that several have compared political freedom (e.g., having civic rights) with free will (choosing one's own path). For example, how much do we conform to others' expectations of us? How much do we really seize the day, as was said long ago? Are we held captive by our beliefs? Do we "think outside the box" enough? Do schools really teach critical thinking skills? What social or commercial practices imprison us? If you read this section with an open mind, you may discover shades of gray mixing with the red, white, and blue...

I disapprove of what you say,
but I will defend to the death your right to say it.

— VOLTAIRE

JASON A. MERCHEY

Peace is possible around the world,
and children are the answer.

— *QUINCY JONES*

I had reasoned this out in my mind, there was one of two
things I had a right to: liberty or death; if I could not have one,
I would have the other.

— *HARRIET TUBMAN*

We will have to understand that, for the common good, we as
individuals will not be able to do everything that we want to do,
whenever and wherever we like, under conditions that only we
can dictate. Instead, we will have to think of the good of the
community, and indeed of the nation, as a whole.

— *SCOTT C. IDLEMAN*

I have been true to the principles of nonviolence, developing a
stronger and stronger aversion to the ideologies of both the far
right and the far left and a deeper sense of rage and sorrow
over the suffering they continue to produce all over the world.

— *JOAN BÁEZ*

I fully share with the President the idea that terrorists must
never be allowed to bring down our love of freedom. I don't
think terrorists ever could. But if we're not careful,
maybe we will do it ourselves.

— *CHARLES SWIFT*

May peace and peace and peace be everywhere.

— *THE UPANISHADS*

Ultimately we have just one moral duty: to reclaim large areas
of peace in ourselves, more and more peace, and to reflect it
toward others. And the more peace there is in us, the more
peace there will be in our troubled world.

— *ETTY HILLESUM*

EIGHT

When what I do, what I think, how I become, flows entirely
from myself, I am free. Self-expression, self-determination
is the essence of freedom.

— MORTIMER J. ADLER

Peace is when time doesn't matter as it passes by.

— MARIA SCHELL

Free will, though it makes evil possible, is also the only thing
that makes possible any love or goodness or joy worth having.
A world of automata – of creatures that worked like machines –
would hardly be worth creating.

— C. S. LEWIS

Peace is not an absence of war. It is a virtue, a state of mind,
a disposition for benevolence, confidence, justice.

— BENEDICT SPINOZA

Last year was the first time I had a Muslim student in my
classroom. She rose and stood silently every morning as the rest
of the class recited the Pledge of Allegiance. After September
11, 2001, she proudly announced one morning that her
mother would now allow her to say the pledge with her
classmates. In one small, third-grade classroom, we dealt
a major blow to al-Qaeda.

— JUDY JOHNSON

Big Brother is watching you.

— GEORGE ORWELL

The women of this nation, in 1876, have greater cause for
discontent, rebellion, and revolution than the men of 1776.

— SUSAN B. ANTHONY

JASON A. MERCHEY

Men fight for liberty and win it with hard knocks. Their
children, brought up easy, let it slip away again, poor fools.
And their grandchildren are once again slaves.

— *D. H. LAWRENCE*

The despotism of custom is everywhere the standing
hindrance to human advancement.

— *JOHN STUART MILL*

I have been sent here with a mandate to assist the Iraqi people
and those responsible for the administration of this land to
achieve freedom, the possibility of managing their own destiny,
and determining their own future.

— *SERGIO VIEIRA DE MELLO*

A Negro had no rights which a white man
was bound to respect...

— *SUPREME COURT DECISION (1857)*

What a delight it is to make friends with
someone you have despised!

— *COLETTE*

...I am poor and naked, but I am the chief of the Nation.
We do not want riches but we do want to train our children
right. Riches would do us no good. We could not take them
with us to the other world. We do not want riches.
We want peace and love.

— *RED CLOUD*

Nothing comes from violence; nothing ever could.

— *STING*

No woman can call herself free until she can choose
consciously whether she will or will not be a mother.

— *MARGARET SANGER*

EIGHT

And if the Supreme Court says that you have the right to consensual sex within your home, then you have the right to bigamy, you have the right to polygamy, you have the right to incest, you have the right to adultery. You have the right to anything. Does that undermine the fabric of our society? I would argue yes, it does. It all comes from, I would argue, this right to privacy that doesn't exist in my opinion in the United States Constitution, this right that was created, it was created in Griswold [the court case]...

— *RICK SANTORUM*

We live in a dirty and dangerous world. There are some things the general public does not need to know, and shouldn't. I believe democracy flourishes when the government can take legitimate steps to keep its secrets and when the press can decide whether to print what it knows.

— *KATHARINE GRAHAM*

I've seen hatred –
it's no way to solve problems and resolve disputes.

— *WESLEY CLARK*

Hero worship is strongest where there is least regard for human freedom.

— *HERBERT SPENCER*

Slowly, as the Old Europeans, for the most part unsuccessfully, try to protect themselves from their barbaric invaders, new definitions of what is normal for both society and ideology begin to emerge. Everywhere now we see the shift in social priorities that is like an arrow shot through time to pierce our age with its nuclear tip: the shift toward more effective technologies of destruction.

— *RIANE EISLER*

JASON A. MERCHEY

When liberty is taken away by force, it can be restored by force.
When it is relinquished voluntarily by default,
it can never be recovered.

— *DOROTHY THOMPSON*

By physical liberty I mean the right to do anything which does
not interfere with the happiness of another; by intellectual
liberty I mean the right to think wrong.

— *ROBERT G. INGERSOLL*

Our choice [of how to respond to the September 11 attacks] is
this: do we want to pursue a path of vengeance, or do we want
to pursue a path that actually leads to a twenty-first century that
all of us can live in?

— *SHARIF ABDULLAH*

They have not wanted *Peace* at all; they have wanted
to be spared war – as though the absence of war was
the same as peace.

— *DOROTHY THOMPSON*

A just war is in the long run far better for a nation's soul than
the most prosperous peace obtained by acquiescence toward
wrong or injustice. Moreover, though it is criminal for a nation
not to prepare for war, so that it may escape the dreadful
consequences of being defeated in war, it must always be
remembered that even to be defeated in war is far better than
never to have fought at all.

— *THEODORE ROOSEVELT*

Nuclear weapons and nuclear energy are medically
contraindicated for all life on earth.

— *HELEN CALDICOTT*

EIGHT

I have come to realize that once we strip radical social
movements down to their bare essence and understand the
collective desires of people in motion, freedom and love lay
at the very heart of the matter.

— *Robin D. G. Kelley*

Today, the military provides much more aggressive
psychological diagnosis and support for veterans, but I can't
help thinking about John Muhammad, the alleged Washington
sniper, whose skills were honed in the Army. War inevitably
breaks minds as well as bodies.

— *Patricia J. Williams*

The United States is not a country to which peace is necessary.

— *Grover Cleveland*

For many, frugality can be a path to liberation…
There is wealth beyond money.

— *Vicki Robin*

To engage in war is always to pick a wild card. And war must
always be a last resort, not a first choice. I truly must question
the judgment of any president who can say that a massive
unprovoked military attack on a nation which is over
50 percent children is "in the highest moral traditions
of our country."

— *Robert Byrd*

We are a free society that cherishes free and unfettered speech.
This of course has consequences.

— *Martin J. Chavez*

Peace is not merely the absence of war,
but the presence of justice.

— *Martin Luther King, Jr.*

JASON A. MERCHEY

I am really too much of an anarchist to bother about all the
trifling details, all I want is freedom, perfect, unrestricted
liberty for myself and others.

— EMMA GOLDMAN

Until humanity evolves significantly, the best way I can envision
for a wealthy person to secure the liberty and safety they prize
is not by saving an extra 5% in revenue, but rather, to
enthusiastically use their influence to force their representatives
to wisely use their 40% in taxes to provide for the education
and safety and justice of our citizens and to conduct American
international affairs with honor, strength, and magnanimity.

— JASON MERCHEY

If one wishes to advocate a free society – that is, capitalism –
one must realize that its indispensable foundation is the
principle of individual rights.

— AYN RAND

I think that we should be men first, and subjects afterward.

— HENRY DAVID THOREAU

What law have I broken? Is it wrong for me to love my own?
Is it wicked because my skin is red? Because I am Sioux?
Because I was born where my fathers lived? Because I would
die for my people and my country?

— SITTING BULL

Anyone who knows history, particularly the history of Europe,
will, I think, recognize that the domination of education or of
government by any one particular religious faith is never a
happy arrangement for the people.

— ELEANOR ROOSEVELT

Give me the liberty to know, to utter, and to argue freely
according to conscience above all liberties.

— JOHN MILTON

EIGHT

The rallying cry of the amazing diversity of organizations that
converged in Seattle in late 1999 was the simple word
"democracy." Democracy flourishes when people organize to
protect their communities and rights and hold their elected
officials accountable.

— *SARAH ANDERSON & JOHN CAVANAGH*

You are a Siddhartha Gautama, made of the same stuff as other
men and women but also as all past and future Siddhartha
Gautamas. There is simply no support for saying women can't
become Siddhartha Gautamas.

— *SIDDHARTHA GAUTAMA*

The strong man condemned by society for doing what his
nature demands will suffer from guilt and self-hatred,
and may well be turned into a criminal.

— *FRIEDRICH NIETZSCHE*

I have witnessed the softening of the hardest of hearts
by a simple smile. Human kindness can turn armaments
into armistice.

— *GOLDIE HAWN*

We may never know the extent to which we are free, but it
seems safe to say that we attribute to ourselves much more
freedom than we actually have.

— *WES NISKER*

Only liberation from archaic authorities of all kinds, in the
views of Thomas Jefferson and Thomas Paine,
would lift the dead hand of the past off the
shoulders of the present generation.

— *JOYCE APPLEBY*

JASON A. MERCHEY

As terrible as 9/11 was, it didn't repeal the Constitution.
— *ROSEMARY POOLER*

I am not a liberator. Liberators do not exist.
The people liberate themselves.
— *CHÉ GUEVARA*

Freedom fighters do not always win, but they are always right.
— *MOLLY IVINS*

If a nation values anything more than freedom,
it will lose its freedom.
— *W. SOMERSET MAUGHAM*

Freedom won through bloodshed or fraud is no freedom.
— *MOHANDAS K. GANDHI*

A liberation movement that is nonviolent sets the oppressor
free as well as the oppressed.
— *BARBARA DEMING*

May the road rise up to meet you.
May the wind always be at your back.
May the sun shine warm upon your face, the rains fall soft upon
your fields, and until we meet again,
may God hold you in the palm of His hand.
— *GAELIC BLESSING*

Human life consists in mutual service. So grief, pain,
misfortune, or "broken heart" is no excuse for cutting off one's
life while any power of service remains. But when all usefulness
is over, when one is assured of an unavoidable and imminent
death, it is the simplest of human rights to choose a quick and
easy death in place of a slow and horrible one.
— *CHARLOTTE PERKINS GILMAN*

A word to the wise – increase the peace.

— PAULY FUEMANA

The Executive Office shall hold no power to unilaterally alter constitutional rights.

— TIMOTHY MCVEIGH

You don't get to choose how you're going to die. Or when. You can only decide how you're going to live. Now.

— JOAN BÁEZ

Trying to be a first-rate reporter on the average American newspaper is like trying to play Bach's 'St. Matthew's Passion' on a ukulele.

— BAGDIKIAN'S OBSERVATION

The rising tide of opposition here and abroad will play into fear mongering and an expansion of government control over citizen rights. There is a kind of proto-fascist dimension to the current set of circumstances. You have this crackdown, coupled with a consolidation of military power and a messianic view that the United States is the bearer of a benevolent future that justifies exterminating those who stand in the way. You have the convergence of religious evangelicals in the White House with geopolitical fundamentalists like Richard Perle and Paul Wolfowitz. We have never had this mixture of religious and secular extremists so close to the core of governmental power.

— RICHARD FALK

You can no more win a war than you can win an earthquake.

— JEANNETTE RANKIN

Liberty means responsibility. That is why most men dread it.

— GEORGE BERNARD SHAW

JASON A. MERCHEY

There is no easy road to freedom.
— *NELSON MANDELA*

If this country continues on its current trajectory toward
becoming a police state, we're going to need a lot more
revolutionaries – from leaders and organizers to people who
are simply ready and able to say, "No" when asked to conform
to something that goes against their humanity.
— *ARIEL GORE*

As I came to power peacefully, so shall I keep it.
— *CORAZON AQUINO*

Peace is always beautiful.
— *WALT WHITMAN*

I don't think we should take any action that should
cause any more loss of life…
— *BARBARA LEE*

You may give children your love but not your thoughts,
for they have their own thoughts.
— *KAHLIL GIBRAN*

One can practice Islam in America without worrying about
secret police dragging people out of bed in the middle of the
night. Women can pray and lecture in American mosques
rather than suffer exclusion from society. In America, one can
criticize the government and feel patriotic. It is not an issue of
being anti-secularism or anti-religion, but of being anti-
oppression and anti-exploitation.
— *MAHER HATHOUT*

EIGHT

I know that in the past every great political and social change,
necessitated violence... Yet it is one thing to employ violence in
combat as a means of defense. It is quite another thing to make
a principle of terrorism, to institutionalize it to assign it the
most vital place in the social struggle. Such terrorism begets
counter-revolution and in turn itself becomes
counter-revolutionary.

— *EMMA GOLDMAN*

To be a true believer, one must be free. To become a believer
under pressure or coercion will not be true belief.

— *ABDOL KARIM SOROUSH*

Peace is not the absence of conflict, but the presence of
creative alternatives for responding to conflict – alternatives
to passive or aggressive responses, alternatives to violence.

— *DOROTHY THOMPSON*

Terror's threat is real. But as we grudgingly grant government
more leeway to guard our lives, we must demand that our
protectors be especially careful to safeguard our rights.

— *WILLIAM SAFIRE*

There are many people who are very religious and who believe
abortion should be an individual decision. The issue is, who
gets to make the choice: will it be you, the government,
or a stranger?

— *SARAH WEDDINGTON*

When the practice of nonviolence becomes universal,
God will reign on earth as He does in heaven.

— *MOHANDAS K. GANDHI*

JASON A. MERCHEY

There will never be a new world order until
women are a part of it.

— *ALICE PAUL*

We have to find room in our contemporary worldview for
persons and all that entails – not just bodies, but *persons*. That
means trying to solve the problem of freedom, finding room
for choice and responsibility, trying to understand individuality.

— *RICHARD LINKLATER*

None who have always been free can understand the terrible,
fascinating power of the hope of freedom to those
who are not free.

— *PEARL S. BUCK*

The earth is the mother of all people, and all people should
have equal rights upon it. You might as well expect the rivers
to run backward as that any man who was born a free man
should be contented when penned up and denied liberty
to go where he pleases.

— *CHIEF JOSEPH*

Adam, poor man! Punished for nothing.

— *ELIE WIESEL*

Humanists recognize that it is only when people feel free to
think for themselves, using reason as their guide, that they are
best capable of developing values that succeed in satisfying
human needs and serving human interests.

— *ISAAC ASIMOV*

Be peaceful, be courteous, obey the law, respect everyone, but
if someone puts a hand on you, send him to the cemetery.

— *MALCOLM X*

Until you've lost your reputation, you never realize
what a burden it was.

— *Margaret Mitchell*

People demand freedom of speech to make up for the freedom
of thought which they avoid.

— *Sören Kierkegaard*

The whole history of the progress of human liberty shows that
all concessions yet made to her august claims have been born
of earnest struggle... If there is no struggle, there is no
progress. Those who profess to favor freedom, and yet
deprecate agitation, are men who want crops without thunder
and lightening. They want the ocean without the awful roar
of its many waters.

— *Frederick Douglass*

Freedom is fragile and must be protected. To sacrifice it,
even as a temporary measure, is to betray it.

— *Germaine Greer*

The soldier, above all other people, prays for peace, for he
must suffer and bear the deepest wounds and scars of war.

— *Douglas MacArthur*

Life is like a coin. You can spend it any way you wish,
but you can only spend it once.

— *Miguel de Cervantes*

Law is nothing unless close behind it stands a warm,
living public opinion.

— *Wendell Phillips*

...Nietzsche referred to *ressentiment*: those who cultivate
humility and the other propitiatory virtues to cloak their
weakness nourish an envious resentment against those stronger
than themselves. They want revenge for their inferiority and
have a deep desire to humiliate and harm.

— *PHILIPPA FOOT*

O, let my land be a land where Liberty
Is crowned with no patriotic wreath,
But opportunity is real, and life is free,
Equality is in the air we breathe.

— *LANGSTON HUGHES*

What better way to fight boxcutter-weilding terrorists than to
order a record number of fighterjets from Lockheed Martin?

— *MICHAEL MOORE*

On the shores of our free states are emerging the poor,
shattered, broken remnants of families – men and women,
escaped, by miraculous providence, from the surges of slavery,
feeble in knowledge, and, in many cases, infirm in moral
constitution, from a system which confounds and confuses
every principle of Christianity and morality. They come to seek
refuge among you; they come to seek education,
knowledge, and Christianity.

— *HARRIET BEECHER STOWE*

Liberty must have been one of humankind's earliest values, for as
soon as humans developed into *Homo sapiens,* and began to speak and
own items, the need to safeguard liberty was primary. Civilization has
been thought of as an exchange of certain liberties for certain benefits,
such as the ability to trade and provide for the common defense.
America's founders had their eyes on how much liberty to grant citizens,
just as some far older cultures held freedom and the sovereignty of the
individual as necessary for "the good society." "The history of liberty is the

EIGHT

history of limitations on the power of the government," as Woodrow Wilson noted. Today is a monumental time for American's civil liberties, as we weigh the ideas of safety versus liberty. Many concessions have already been made, many tethers attached to the human being by various institutions. I maintain that a government that protects us well and provides humanitarian support for those in need does not have to encroach on a person's autonomy to do so. For example, burning one at the stake for not believing the true religion is not an acceptable usurpation of liberty, but instead was the church unjustly controlling the individual. We must be wary of such concessions and reserve no passion or means in doing so. It is worth noting, however, that if we are to demand freedom, we must accept a stout responsibility. Oftentimes, when one says he wishes to have liberty, what he means is he wants to be left alone to pursue dishonorable actions; a child molester does not have an authentic right to freedom to perform acts he has a penchant for. John Milton informs us on this aspect of liberty: "License they mean when they cry 'Liberty,' for who loves that must first be wise and good."

CHAPTER NINE

KINDNESS, MAGNANIMITY, & ALTRUISM

This chapter is one of the loftiest and worthiest elements of the values of the wise. Though we may not use these words very often, they describe what I believe to be the brighter side of humanity. To me, kindness connotes ideas such as "goodness," "love," "benevolence," and "compassion." Prophets and saints and even Jesus of Nazareth often had the word "benevolent" used to describe them, and what they exemplified is not beyond the reach of any of us. Altruism is controversial because it is so easily confused with a "self-serving service to others." However, an altruistic act is one in which one risks one's self to help another. Both those who put themselves in danger to rescue Nazi victims in World War II as well as those who rushed into the collapsing World Trade Center exemplified heroic and selfless acts that can be described as nothing other than altruism. Others of us may walk away from a person in need, only later realizing that what we "ought to have done" was the harder, more loving thing. The wonderful words in this section inspire us to believe in the possibility that we too can rise to heights we rarely imagine. Or simply be kind to others every single day.

A bone to the dog is not charity. Charity is the bone shared with the dog when you are just as hungry as the dog.

— JACK LONDON

JASON A. MERCHEY

I don't know of anybody in my home town who is destitute;
I wouldn't let them be.

— LILLIAN CARTER

From what we get, we can make a living; what we give,
however, makes a life.

— ARTHUR ASHE

I believe that what truly matters in the making of art is not what
the final piece looks like or sounds like, not what it is worth or
not worth, but what newness gets added to the universe in the
process of the piece itself becoming.

— JAN PHILLIPS

I'm not a professional philanthropist, and I'm not running
for sainthood. I just happen to think that in life we need to be
a little like the farmer who puts back into the soil what
he takes out.

— PAUL NEWMAN

There is no such thing as other people's children.

— HILLARY RODHAM CLINTON

Capital punishment…has always been a religious punishment
and is irreconcilable with humanism.

— ALBERT CAMUS

It was the custom to provide for the old and the sick. There was
always room in the safety and warmth of *la familia* for one
more person, be that person a stranger or a friend.

— RUDOLFO A. ANAYA

As for Jesus being a socialist, I take it back. He was actually a
little to the left of that, judging from his instruction to the rich
man to sell all that he had and give to the poor.

— BARBARA EHRENREICH

142

NINE

We are at a crossroads; I am at a crossroads; you are at a crossroads. We are in the midst of an age-old story, that of the forces of light versus the forces of darkness. Will we choose the path of fear, anger, and revenge, or will we choose the path of nonviolence and hope?

— MICHAEL TOMS

We have to extend this enormous wealth that we have, this economic wealth we have in a few countries, and be measured by how generous we are. I think we have to stop this xenophobia. We have to rethink some of our institutions. What are we teaching young people in American business schools? Are they just developing the same status quo, this belief that maximizing profits and accumulation of wealth is all that matters? Maybe what is needed now is a real change in education that embraces not a religious education, but a spiritual education.

— ANITA RODDICK

Don't complain about what you don't have. Use what you've got. To do less than your best is a sin. Every single one of us has the power for greatness, because greatness is determined by service – to yourself and to others.

— OPRAH WINFREY

Who are you that men should rend their bosom and unveil their pride, that you may see their worth naked and their pride unabashed? See first that you yourself deserve to be a giver, an instrument of giving – for in truth, it is life that gives unto life – while you who deem yourself a giver are but a witness.

— KAHLIL GIBRAN

Hungry people cannot be good at learning or producing anything, except perhaps violence.

— PEARL BAILEY

JASON A. MERCHEY

It is high time the ideal of success should be replaced
with the ideal of service.

— *ALBERT EINSTEIN*

Make kindness your daily *modus operandi*
and change your world.

— *ANNIE LENNOX*

Sharing what's valuable in life means not just giving away
material goods, but also time, attention, wisdom, and energy –
the things that create a strong, rich, and diverse community.

— *SCOTT FARRELL*

May I allay the suffering of every living being; I am the
medicine for the sick; may I be both the doctor and the
nurse until the sickness does not recur.

— *SHANTIDEVA*

The Eskimos don't believe in competition.
They don't believe in envy. They believe in sharing.

— *JUDY WICKS*

Why were we able to put hundreds of thousands of troops and
support personnel in Saudi Arabia within a few months to fight
Saddam Hussein when we are unable to mobilize hundreds of
teachers or doctors and nurses and social workers for
desperately underserved inner cities and rural areas to fight the
tyranny of poverty and ignorance and child neglect and abuse?

— *MARIAN WRIGHT EDELMAN*

I now perceive an immense omission in my psychology –
the deepest principle of human nature is the
craving to be appreciated.

— *WILLIAM JAMES*

CHAPTER NINE

Out of the experience of an extraordinary human disaster
that lasted too long must be born a society of which
humanity will be proud.
— *NELSON MANDELA*

The legacy of a man is created through a few
remarkable situations.
What honor lies in philosophizing from one's
soporific armchair?
'Tis a world full of pessimists, of mutable morals –
Indeed, those who show greatness are becoming
increasingly rare.
— *JASON MERCHEY*

From the ashes of destruction, I hope the outpouring of
kindness and commitment that arose after 9/11/2001
continues. There could be no better monument than
increasing our positive intentions and actions toward our fellow
human beings. This has the power to change the world.
Let the difference begin with us.
— *CATHRYN GOLDEN*

Mistrust your zeal for doing good to others.
— *ABBE HUVELIN*

My main goal when I retired was to give back.
— *GIGI FERNÁNDEZ*

It's not the circumstances you come from;
it's the values you fight for.
— *JOHN F. KERRY*

We must learn to love each other as brothers
or perish together as fools.
— *MARTIN LUTHER KING, JR.*

JASON A. MERCHEY

Great men are always linked to their age by
some weakness or other.
— *JOHANN WOLFGANG VON GOETHE*

I believe that man will not merely endure; he will prevail.
He is immortal, not because he alone among creatures has an
inexhaustible voice, but because he has a soul, a spirit capable
of compassion and sacrifice and endurance.
— *WILLIAM FAULKNER*

One of the signs of passing youth is the birth of a sense of
fellowship with other human beings as we take our place
among them.
— *VIRGINIA WOOLF*

I consider myself a Hindu, Christian, Moslem, Jew,
Buddhist, and Confucian.
— *MOHANDAS K. GANDHI*

From my early childhood I have heard the United States of
America, my country, being referred to as a "Christian" nation.
Jesus preached, "Love your neighbor" and, "Turn the other
cheek" and, "You're your enemies." The U.S. government has
not been behaving as if it represents a "Christian" nation.
— *MICHAEL TOMS*

God will not force us to do good. You must choose to do good.
— *MOTHER TERESA*

The best time to plant a tree is 20 years ago.
The second best time is now.
— *CHINESE PROVERB*

Giving a kidney is the coolest thing I've ever done
and if I had a spare, I'd do it again.
— *CHRISTINE KARG-PALREIRO*

NINE

So soon as prudence has begun to grow up in the brain,
like a dismal fungus, it finds its first expression in a paralysis
of generous acts.

— ROBERT LOUIS STEVENSON

The time is always right to do what's right.

— MARTIN LUTHER KING, JR.

Five decades of study by the Disaster Research Center at the
University of Delaware seems to indicate that humans, even in
traumatic situations, tend toward altruism rather than
selfishness. Perhaps we are more altruistic at our core than
our day-to-day selfishness would indicate.

— LEE CLARK & JACQUELINE WHITE

You can have the most exciting time in human history, but we
have to defeat people who think they can find their
redemption in our destruction. Then we have to be smart
enough to get rid of our arrogant self-righteousness so that we
don't claim for ourselves things that we deny for others. Then
in the end, we've got to be able to stand up and say, "We are
not against Islam, but we want to have a clear understanding
about what we think is the nature of truth, the value of life,
and the content of community."

— WILLIAM JEFFERSON CLINTON

He who will not open the door to give alms will
open it for the doctor.

— HINDU PROVERB

America is an enormous frosted cupcake in the middle of
millions of starving people.

— GLORIA STEINEM

Brotherhood is the very price and condition of man's survival.

— CARLOS P. ROMULO

JASON A. MERCHEY

A pat on the back, though only a few vertebrae removed from a
kick in the pants, is miles ahead in results.
— *BENNETT CERF*

Give me your tired, your poor, your huddled masses yearning to
breathe free, the wretched refuse of your teeming shores; send
these, the homeless, tempest-tossed to me,
I lift my lamp beside the golden door.
— *EMMA LAZARUS*

You can't leave footprints in the sands of time by sitting down.
— *KARL BURNS*

Cherishing children is the mark of a civilized society.
— *JOAN G. COONEY*

Regarding liberal concern for the world's disfranchised, I think
that on a small scale it is helpful – if not altruistic. However,
regarding guilt about not being able to help everyone, do
everything, and change the way the system works, I would say
this: be part of the solution and not part of the problem and
you can feel good enough (though not great). You and I are
not the originators of luck. We are not the designer of the
universe, nor do we have the power to manipulate complex
sociological phenomena with a simple benevolent thought.
Live consciously and hope that the darker side of human
nature does not ruin this experiment that's been
running for the last 20,000 years.
— *JASON MERCHEY*

You can give money, you can give service,
but body parts are another thing.
— *REEDA KRAVINSKY*

CHAPTER

NINE

America's special role in the world – its ability to buck history –
is based not simply on its great strength, but on a global faith
that this power is legitimate. If America squanders that, the loss
will outweigh any gains in domestic security. And this next
American century could prove to be lonely, brutish and short.
— *FAREED ZAKARIA*

[There are more than two-and-a-quarter million U.S. citizens in
prison in 2003] – it's by far the highest per capita prison
population of the Western countries – and it's gone way up
because the 1994 Crime Bill was extremely harsh. Furthermore,
the prisons in the United States are so inhumane by this
point that they are being condemned by international human
rights organizations as literally imposing torture.
— *NOAM CHOMSKY*

If anyone has hurt me or harmed me knowingly or
unknowingly in thought, word, or deed, I freely forgive them.
And I too ask forgiveness if I have hurt anyone or harmed
anyone knowingly or unknowingly in thought, word, or deed.
— *SIDDHARTHA GAUTAMA*

Believe, when you are most unhappy, that there is something
for you to do in the world. So long as you can sweeten
another's pain, life is not in vain.
— *HELEN KELLER*

Dearest Lord, teach me to be generous.
— *IGNATIUS LOYOLA*

They who give have all things; they who withhold have nothing.
— *HINDU PROVERB*

JASON A. MERCHEY

The crucial test for liberal democracies is to prove that they
have the proper instruments to effect empathy, caring,
and freedom for transforming social, political, and
economic institutions.

— *MARCUS G. RASKIN*

The heroes we need to celebrate should be men and women,
but particularly men, who root themselves in connection rather
than separation, and who measure their achievement by
standards of care as much as individual accomplishment.

— *PEARL M. OLINER & SAMUEL P. OLINER*

This is how we were warned it would be. President Reagan told
us from the very beginning that he believed in a kind of social
Darwinism – survival of the fittest – government can't do
everything we were told, so it should settle for taking care of
the strong and hope that economic ambition and charity will
do the rest. Make the rich richer, and what falls from the table
will be enough for the middle class and those who are trying
desperately to work their way into the middle class.

— *MARIO CUOMO*

Almsgiving tends to perpetuate poverty;
aid does away with it once and for all.

— *EVA PERÓN*

Charity is fruitful only when we feel the three pure feelings:
feeling joy before the gift is given; giving gracefully; and having
pleasure of it after; that is perfect charity.

— *SIDDHARTHA GAUTAMA*

The idea of doing good for others in order to feel good
yourself makes sense for many people. But this is not
why altruists act as they do.

— *KRISTEN RENWICK MONROE*

CHAPTER

NINE

We make sure the people have proper daycare, that they have assistance for their parents when they're elderly and need to be in an old-age home, that they have proper health care that insures they won't lose their business or their house because they can't afford their medical bills...
that's how you build a good society.
— MIKE BRADLEY

Hatred is a feeling which leads to the extinction of values.
— JOSÉ ORTEGA Y GASSET

Blessed are those who can give without remembering,
and take without forgetting.
— ELIZABETH BIBESCO

The best practical advice I can give to the present generation is to practice the virtue which the Christians call love.
— BERTRAND RUSSELL

Pity may represent little more than the impersonal concern which prompts the mailing of a check, but true sympathy is the personal concern which demands the giving of one's soul.
— MARTIN LUTHER KING, JR.

Compassion is the natural response of the heart unclouded by the specious view that we are separate from one another.
— SYLVIA BOORSTEIN

Is there no bright reversion in the sky
For those who greatly think, or greatly die?
— ALEXANDER POPE

On the whole, human beings want to be good,
but not too good, and not quite all the time.
— GEORGE ORWELL

...the world needs healers, not artists.

— *JANE ARDEN*

It is true that there has been an outpouring of benevolence since September 11; it is natural for members of a community to come together in a crisis. But it is not true that human nature is essentially good or that evil is rare. And it is the worst kind of wishful thinking to believe otherwise.

— *JEFF JACOBY*

I come to present the strong claims of suffering humanity. I come to place before the Legislature of Massachusetts the condition of the miserable, the desolate, the outcast. I come as the advocate of helpless, forgotten, insane men and women; of beings sunk to a condition from which the unconcerned world would start with real horror.

— *DOROTHEA DIX*

[For those who deny God's existence], if someone comes to you and asks your help, you shall not turn him away with pious words, saying: "Have faith and take your troubles to God!" You shall act as if there were no God, and as if there were only one person in all the world who could help this man – only yourself.

— *MOSHE LIEB*

The spectacle of the Christians loving all men was the most astounding Rome had ever seen.

— *JANE ADDAMS*

I have wondered why Jews praise Abraham for his willingness to murder his son when God commanded it. A true hero who believed in a God who rewards and punishes would have resisted that unjust command and risked God's wrath, just as a true hero would have refused God's order to murder "heathen" women and children during the barbaric crusades.

— *ALAN M. DERSHOWITZ*

America's inner contradiction was the altruist-collectivist ethic. Altruism is incompatible with freedom, with capitalism, and with individual rights. One cannot combine the pursuit of happiness with the moral status of a sacrificial animal.

— *Ayn Rand*

Any life that is lost in war is a human life, be it that of an Arab or an Israeli...

— *Anwar Sadat*

Virtues transcend time and culture (although their cultural expression may vary); justice and kindness, for example, will always and everywhere be virtues, regardless of how many people exhibit them.

— *Thomas Lickona*

When will our consciences grow so tender that we will act to prevent human misery rather than avenge it?

— *Eleanor Roosevelt*

Compassion and kindness as the basis of our relationship with nonhuman fellow beings means "doing no harm."

— *Vandana Shiva*

Tell me I've led a good life; tell me I am a good man.

— *Robert Rodat*

Everybody would like to know that they had an impact and they were part of something that was important.

— *Sarah Weddington*

As Treasury chief, Paul O'Neill has said that Social Security and Medicare are not necessary. Perhaps that's because he receives an annual pension from Alcoa of $926,000.

— *Michael Moore*

JASON A. MERCHEY

Man's most human characteristic is not his ability to learn,
which he shares with many other species, but his ability to teach
and store what others have developed and taught him.
— *MARGARET MEAD*

My religion is very simple. My religion is kindness.
— *TENZIN GYATSO*

Competition and individualism appear to be basic human
needs, and society benefits from them. But they need to be
tempered and balanced by care.
— *PEARL M. OLINER & SAMUEL P. OLINER*

The moral test of government is how that government treats
those who are in the dawn of life, the children; those who are
in the twilight of life, the elderly; and those who are in the
shadows of life, the sick, the needy, and the handicapped.
— *HUBERT HUMPHREY*

If enough people consider compassion to be important, then
the world becomes a more compassionate place.
— *PHIL CATALFO*

Charity is a virtue of attachment, and the sympathy for others
which makes it easier to help them is part of the virtue itself.
— *PHILIPPA FOOT*

If I can't love Hitler, I can't love at all.
— *A. J. MUSTE*

We women have great influence, and we need to become
warriors of peace, guardians of love, and agents of kindness.
The result can only be the great satisfaction of creating
happiness, and this is contagious.
— *ADRIANA DE GASPAR DE ALBA*

I imagine a world of kindness to be a place where it is
Christmas 365 days of the year – where the magic cast by our
volunteers is found everywhere, every day, and compassion
is the universal response to homelessness.

— SHAKS GHOSH

Ask yourself: have you been kind today?
Was anyone kind to you? How did it feel?

— ANNIE LENNOX

For all their invocations of God, it seems that the right's moral
missionaries had only read every other page of the Bible –
ignoring the incessant warnings in both testaments about the
evils of becoming obsessed with riches and growing callous
toward the less fortunate.

— DAVID CALLAHAN

We humans have the capacity to change the world with acts
of love and kindness. Let's start by teaching our children
the importance of compassion.

— GOLDIE HAWN

What is violence? Bullets, nightsticks, and fists are not the only
forms of violence. It is also violence when people ignore the
fact that infants are starving in one corner of our city.

— SEHUI CHO

As the sun makes the ice melt, kindness causes
misunderstanding, mistrust, and hostility to evaporate.

— ALBERT SCHWEITZER

JASON A. MERCHEY

The remarkable thing about magnanimity, which comes from the Latin words *magna* and *animus* meaning "great spirit," is that it involves a fusion of such astounding beauty and strength. Another facet of the idea of magnanimity is that it benefits everyone who is within ten feet. For example, when a person gives to one who is really needy, it makes his or her own world brighter, it evokes a positive feeling in the giver, and the young child of the generous person is likely to learn by his mother's act of kindness to a stranger. The essence of magnanimity is to do the strong, helpful, "classy" thing, even if doing so is not easy. It's the thing that movie heroes are made of, when they don't succumb to the desire to behead the bad guy because to do so would be "stooping to their level." It is the judge who says, "This is your first offense; I'm going to let you off with probation this time." If someone cuts you off in traffic and you think to yourself, "You must be in a hurry" rather than, "Screw you, buddy!" you are living this sublime value. Finally, it is worth emphasizing that being magnanimous is not easy – it is a labor of love. Some do not understand the suppleness evident in the magnanimous person, for it appears to be weakness instead. Indeed, as Albert Einstein, who was termed by some a "great spirit," noted: "Great spirits have always encountered violent opposition from mediocre minds."

SELF-CONFIDENCE
& SELF-WORTH

If the virtue of modesty pulls one's self-image toward the ground, the value self-worth raises it toward the sky. The idea behind self-worth is to make as high an appraisal of one's self as one truly can. It is an abiding belief in what one is made of deep down inside. Wisdom in action is to forget about what others think, even if they are critical of *you*. Would history's greatest known characters ever have attempted or succeeded in their visions and goals if they defeated themselves because of faltering self-worth? On the contrary, it is likely that some people would do well to temper their self-image with a little modesty. However, the challenge for me as a human being, which is highlighted by the work I ask my clients in psychotherapy to do, is: How do I find more self-confidence and self-worth? How do I raise my self-esteem? These questions are an important part of *a life of value*, since self-confidence and self-worth make life more worth living and bring an array of opportunities within grasp.

I find the statement "You can't" offensive to the human spirit. We can be anything.

— *MAYA ANGELOU*

Never esteem anything as of advantage to thee that shall make thee break thy word or lose thy self-respect.

— *MARCUS AURELIUS*

When no one else is visible, it doesn't mean no one is around; I am still here. A witness might notice me doing something wrong, but I see it much more deeply.

— *SIDDHARTHA GAUTAMA*

It occurred to me when I was thirteen and wearing white gloves and Mary Janes and going to dancing school, that no one should have to dance backward all their lives.

— *JILL RUCKELSHAUS*

The cultural firestorm around the yuppies was so intense because they hijacked the new individualism and took it in a sharply materialistic direction.

— *DAVID CALLAHAN*

I'm no lady; I'm a member of Congress, and I'll proceed on that basis.

— *MARY NORTON*

People who know how much is enough have everything they want and need to live a life *defined by themselves* as fulfilling and meaningful. They have a purpose for their lives larger than simply meeting their individual needs.

— *VICKI ROBIN*

Only when faced with the activity of enemies can you learn real inner strength. From this viewpoint, even enemies are teachers of inner strength, courage, and determination.

— *TENZIN GYATSO*

Most people, after one success, are so cringingly afraid of doing less well that they rub all the edge off their subsequent work.

— *Beatrix Potter*

This time, vote for what you believe in.

— *Paul Wellstone*

What exactly is success? For me it is to be found not in applause, but in the satisfaction of feeling that one is realizing one's ideal.

— *Anna Pavlova*

No one can harm the man who does himself no wrong.

— *St. John Chrysostom*

How can a tyrant rule the free and the proud, but for a tyranny in their own freedom and a shame in their own pride?

— *Kahlil Gibran*

If one cannot state a matter clearly enough so that even an intelligent twelve-year-old can understand it, one should remain within the cloistered walls of the university and laboratory until one gets a better grasp of one's subject matter.

— *Margaret Mead*

Alone and afraid in a world we never made, we often yearn for marching orders from a superior power whose greater authority will direct our energies while making us feel sure that they are being properly used.

— *Irving Singer*

Think wrongly, if you please, but in all cases think for yourself.

— *Doris Lessing*

That fear created the gods is perhaps as true as anything
so brief could be on so great a subject.

— GEORGE SANTYANA

We have much more power than perhaps we realize to direct
our financial resources in ways that support, empower, and
express what we believe in. It takes courage to direct the flow,
but with each choice, we invest in the world as we envision it.

— LYNNE TWIST

Get up, stand up – stand up for your rights!
Get up, stand up, never give up the fight!

— BOB MARLEY

I want to stand by my country, but I cannot vote for war.
I vote no.

— JEANNETTE RANKIN

Compassion for yourself translates into compassion for others.

— SUKI JAY MUNSELL

You've got to think that you're something special; otherwise,
how would you tolerate all the crap you have to go through?

— ROD STEIGER

You can't change the music of your soul.

— KATHARINE HEPBURN

I hope it will not be irreverent for me to say that if it is
probable that God would reveal his will to others, on a point so
connected to my duty, it might be supposed that he would
reveal it directly to me… These are not, however, the days of
miracles… I must study the plain, physical facts of the case,
ascertain what is possible, and learn what appears
to be wise and right.

— ABRAHAM LINCOLN

I've taught my children that nobody is going to help them –
they've got to do it for themselves. If you want to get
somewhere in life, it's up to you. Despite the prejudice
and nit-picking, you can still do it if you really want to.
— *MYRTLE FAYE RUMPH*

The first prerogative of an artist in any medium
is to make a fool of himself.
— *PAULINE KAEL*

What is a rebel? A man who says, "No."
— *ALBERT CAMUS*

Don't bow before another person or another nation.
— *MOHANDAS K. GANDHI*

The public somebody you are when you have a "name" is a
fiction... The only somebody worth being is the solitary and
unseen you that existed from your first breath and which is the
sum of your actions...
— *TENNESSEE WILLIAMS*

Always hold firmly to the thought that each one of us can do
something to bring some portion of misery to an end.
— *BONNIE ACKER*

Joy for me is finally being able to define boundaries for myself
– which I had never done before. In other words, letting your
yes be yes and your no be no, and not feeling guilty or bad
about any of it.
— *RENE RUSSO*

Let him not be another's who can be his own.
— *THEOPHRASTUS PARACELSUS*

JASON A. MERCHEY

In our nation, the people are sovereign, not the government.
It is the people, not the media or the financial system or
megacorporations or the two political parties, who have
the power to create change.

— *HOWARD DEAN*

Do not be led by rumor, or tradition, or hearsay. Do not be led
by the authority of religious scripture, nor by simple logic or
inference, nor by mere appearance, nor by the pleasure of
speculation, nor by vague possibilities, nor by respect for
"Our Teacher."

— *SIDDHARTHA GAUTAMA*

"Enoughness" – a stance of material sufficiency and spiritual
affluence – describes a transformative way of living that
liberates humans to live in wholeness and balance. When we
are blind to the truth of money, we glimpse "enoughness" and
think we see deprivation. When we open our eyes to the hidden
costs of money – to ourselves and life – we become inspired
generators of human wealth.

— *VICKI ROBIN*

I'm a good person. I'm a good man.

— *ANTWONE FISHER*

[George Orwell] took some of the supposedly Christian virtues
and showed how they could be "lived" without piety
or religious beliefs.

— *CHRISTOPHER HITCHENS*

We don't know who we are until we see what we can do.

— *MARTHA GRIMES*

TEN

There are many who are living far below their possibilities because they are continually handing over their individualities to others. Do you want to be a power in the world? Then be yourself. Be true to the highest within your soul, and then allow yourself to be governed by no customs or conventionalities or arbitrary man-made rules that are not founded on principle.

— *Ralph Waldo Emerson*

It's not so much that we're afraid of change or so in love with the old ways, but it's that place in between that we fear… It's like being between trapezes. It's Linus when his blanket is in the dryer; there's nothing to hold on to.

— *Marilyn Ferguson*

In France if you're part of the intellectual elite and you cough, there's a front-page story about it in *Le Monde*. That's one of the reasons why French intellectual culture is so farcical – it's like Hollywood.

— *Noam Chomsky*

No man is great enough or wise enough for any of us to surrender our destiny to. The only way in which anyone can lead us is to restore to us the belief in our own guidance.

— *Henry Miller*

Never bend your head. Hold it high.
Look the world straight in the eye.

— *Helen Keller*

It's taken me time to understand that there will always be someone who opposes me. I have had to learn to be a little more thick-skinned, yet not become an insensitive armadillo.

— *Federico F. Peña*

JASON A. MERCHEY

Those who are completely satisfied with their accomplishments
have outlived their usefulness.

— *John A. Marshall*

If you think you're too small to make a difference,
you've never been in bed with a mosquito.

— *Anita Roddick*

Blessed are they who heal us of self-despising. Of all services
which can be done to man, I know of none more precious.

— *William Hale White*

Always be a first-rate version of yourself, instead of a
second-rate version of somebody else.

— *Judy Garland*

Happiness depends upon ourselves.

— *Aristotle*

To swallow and follow, whether old doctrine or new
propaganda, is a weakness still dominating the human mind.

— *Charlotte Perkins Gilman*

The closing years of life are like the end of a masquerade party,
when the masks are dropped.

— *Arthur Schopenhauer*

I don't know the key to success, but the key to failure
is trying to please everybody.

— *Bill Cosby*

Jimmy taught me a long time ago that you do the best you can
and don't worry about the criticisms. Once you accept the fact
that you're not perfect you develop some confidence.

— *Rosalynn Carter*

TEN

Make the best use of what is in your power,
and take the rest as it happens.
— *EPICTETUS*

The thing to do, when one feels sure that he has said or done
the right thing, and is condemned, is to stand still and keep
quiet. If he is right, time will show it.
— *BOOKER T. WASHINGTON*

No man can produce great things who is not thoroughly
sincere in dealing with himself.
— *JAMES RUSSELL LOWELL*

We're all in this together – by ourselves.
— *LILY TOMLIN*

Believe nothing no matter where you read it, or who said it –
even if I have said it – unless it agrees with your own reason and
your own common sense.
— *SIDDHARTHA GAUTAMA*

On the dating scene, a guy's confidence can be the key to his
attractiveness. And real confidence means not being afraid to
show your flaws, vulnerabilities, or imperfections. Before I'd
even let my dates into my car, I'd flash them a confident smile
and say, "Hey baby, I hope you're ready for a long night of
painfully narcissistic introspection punctuated by physical
unwieldiness building up to a big, impotent crescendo,
followed by me weeping in a locked bathroom."
— *DENNIS MILLER*

If you don't like something, change it. If you can't change it,
change your attitude.
— *MAYA ANGELOU*

JASON A. MERCHEY

It's lack of faith that makes people afraid of meeting
challenges, and I believe in myself.
— MUHAMMAD ALI

I don't mind living in a man's world
as long as I can be a woman in it.
— MARILYN MONROE

My mind to me a kingdom is;
Such present joys therein I find
That it excels all other bliss
That earth affords or grows by kind.
— EDWARD DYER

Literature is strewn with the wreckage of those who have
minded beyond reason the opinion of others.
— VIRGINIA WOOLF

Life is like a game of cards. The hand that is dealt you
represents determinism; the way you play it is free will.
— JAWAHARLAL NEHRU

Do well, and dread no shame.
— SCOTTISH PROVERB

I am not going to question your opinions.
I am not going to meddle with your belief.
I am not going to dictate to you mine.
All that I say is, examine, inquire.
Look into the nature of things.
Search out the grounds of your opinions, the for and against.
Know why you believe, understand what you believe,
and possess a reason for the faith that is in you.
— FRANCES WRIGHT

A stout man's heart breaks bad luck.
— MIGUEL DE CERVANTES

While you're saving your face you're losing your ass.
— LYNDON JOHNSON

Do not rely completely on any other human being, however dear. We meet all life's greatest tests alone.
— AGNES MACPHAIL

Only he can command who has the courage to disobey.
— WILLIAM McDOUGALL

I am so hip, even my errors are correct.
— NIKKI GIOVANNI

Don't believe a teaching just because you heard it from a man who is supposed to be holy, or because it is contained in a book that is supposed to be holy, or because all your friends and neighbors believe it. Whatever you observe and analyze and found to be reasonable and good, accept that, and put it into practice.
— SIDDHARTHA GAUTAMA

I'm the first to admit that I always prefer approval over disapproval. It feels better and it's certainly easier to deal with. The more content I've become, however, the less I depend on it for my sense of well-being.
— RICHARD CARLSON

It's so hard to find...people who crave intellectualism but also know how to have a good time. My fantasy man has always been a poet on a motorcycle.
— LUCINDA WILLIAMS

Every head must do its own thinking.
— *JABO PROVERB*

I have tried to function as a trusting person and I've been
nailed. Now it's me that I don't trust.
— *CARRIE FISHER*

National leaders who find themselves wilting under the
withering criticisms by members of the media, would do well
not to take such criticism personally but to regard the media as
their allies in keeping the government clean and honest, its
services efficient and timely, and its commitment to democracy
strong and unwavering.
— *CORAZON AQUINO*

We are so vain that we even care for the opinion
of those we don't care for.
— *MARIE EBNER VON ESCHENBACH*

Hope for miracles but don't rely on one.
— *YIDDISH PROVERB*

I hate quotations. Tell me what you know.
— *RALPH WALDO EMERSON*

It is a common delusion that you make things better
by talking about them.
— *DAME ROSE MACAULAY*

He that lives upon hope will die fasting.
— *BENJAMIN FRANKLIN*

Trying to please is always costly.
— *YIDDISH PROVERB*

To do just the opposite is a form of imitation.

— *Georg Christoph Lichtenberg*

If I couldn't be beautiful, I decided I would be smart.

— *Karen Horney*

Wholeheartedness will pierce a rock.

— *Japanese proverb*

Are you, like me, angry that the more I educate myself the less faith I have that any one man is a paragon of honor? That there really are women out there who can be trusted, who are steadfast, and principled? So what if you learn that an old fable is merely aspirational, or that a historical figure was a hypocrite. Fear not: once the words have been said, once a deed is done, it is written not on the sand of a beach, but the sands of time. All you have to do is believe in an ideal, and it is yours. Einstein doesn't own charity; if you see a homeless person, give him a dollar. If you see a politician spout off a phrase about justice – live with justice. Then the virtue is yours, permanently and fully. We can all be heroes the moment we choose to be so.

— *Jason Merchey*

I became an agnostic because traditional Western religions required that I betray my mind. Other belief systems seemed either to require that I betray my body or my heart. For years, I did nothing until it occurred to me one day that I might celebrate the earth, the universe, and myself in ritual and study exactly as other religions did but without their dogma. Thus, I am a pagan, but a pagan whose worship is celebratory rather than "magical."

— *Sandra Fiske*

JASON A. MERCHEY

I've always felt it was not up to anyone else
to make me give my best.
— AKEEM OLAJUWON

In my long life I had to face some difficult decisions and found
myself often in doubt whether I had acted the right way.
— EDWARD TELLER

Big doesn't necessarily mean better.
Sunflowers aren't better than violets.
— EDNA FERBER

If you don't like the style of others, cultivate your own.
— GEORGE KONRAD

We want freedom from the white man rather than to be
integrated. We don't want any part of the establishment, we
want to be free to raise our children in our religion, in our
ways, to be able to hunt and fish and live in peace. We don't
want power, we don't want to be congressmen, or bankers... we
want to be ourselves. We want to have our heritage, because we
are the owners of this land and because we belong here.
— GRAND COUNCIL OF THE AMERICAN INDIANS

To a great extent, raising children who will contribute to society
in positive ways involves helping them to find themselves
and to like what they find.
— SUSAN VOGT

The culture we have does not make people feel good about
themselves. We're teaching the wrong things. And you have to
be strong enough to say, If the culture doesn't work,
don't buy it. Create your own.
— MORRIE SCHWARTZ

Beware of mob mentality. That's what I fear most, and it can
take over in seconds. Hold on to your instincts, hold on
to your liberty, and just continue to stay in that place
of reflection and resolve.

— *INGE KURTZ*

Success, recognition, and conformity are the bywords of the
modern world, where everyone seems to crave the
anesthetizing security of being identified with the majority.

— *MARTIN LUTHER KING, JR.*

Once I knew how to read, I was off on my own.

— *DENNIS KUCINICH*

We never know how high we are
'Till we are called to rise;
And then, if we are true to plan,
Our statures touch the skies.

— *EMILY DICKINSON*

Abide at the center of your being, for the more you leave it,
the less you learn.

— *LAO TZU*

The values in this chapter are some of the most relevant to our
lives because every second of every waking minute each of us is "looking
through our own eyes" out onto the world. In other words, one's feelings
about one's self (*self-confidence*), and one's appraisal of one's self (*self-
worth*) color the way that person interacts with others, makes decisions,
and generally feels about life. The person with higher levels of self-
confidence is likely to be successful in his profession or avocation, to have
less stress, and be involved in more functional and rewarding
relationships. We all know how it feels to doubt one's self; for even the
most successful people experience challenges in their love lives, and
the most beautiful have challenges with confidence that can be

formidable (ask a supermodel!). To live wisely is to attempt to build self-esteem – even as an adult. Our parents and society lay the foundations for our senses of self, and as we grow we take increasing responsibility for growing into the most confident people we can be. Life is full of little moments of choice in which one can face anxiety and act in service of the self – or be pushed around by others and made to go where chance sends them. Learning to live deliberately and with confidence as well as knowing how to love one's self and to be consistently happy – although not always easy – are fundamental to happiness and fulfillment. Indeed, it is much like oiling a noisy axle on an automobile – it takes time and energy to do it, but if one must travel the distance (life) with *or without* efficiency and quiet, why not choose to make the journey as pleasant as possible and make the effort?

CHAPTER ELEVEN

DEVELOPMENT, PROGRESSIVISM, & INTEGRATION

Development is similar to progressivism, though they have slightly different applications. Development describes the course an individual takes toward the better and more sophisticated. Progressivism is the path society takes to grow better and more sophisticated. Change is inevitable, so a person and a people ought to be ready and willing to bring it on. The desire to see the world improve and to bring out our best qualities, such as tolerance, liberty, and justice, is progressivism in action. Integration may be considered to have emerged from the ancient concept of the yin-yang. Integrating the opposites, such as dark/light, anima/animus, emotion/thought, and good/bad is a challenge for every one of us, because humans like to categorize in black and white. When we merge or combine the parts of ourselves with the information out there in the world, we set ourselves upon the path of development and progress. The following quotations highlight the goals, the challenges, and the need for further human evolution. These wise thoughts inspire us to be open to change and offer us a more dynamic picture of what progress is really all about. I want to become the greatest person I can, and I long for our country and our world to meet their potentials as well.

Our greatest foes, and whom we must chiefly combat, are within.
— MIGUEL DE CERVANTES

JASON A. MERCHEY

There is no way of improving anything until one has learned
how to improve one's self.
— PHYLLIS BOTTOME

We stand on the shoulders of our ancestors no matter how
many machines we invent. Only our memory and our
metaphors carry us forward, not our money, our gadgets,
or our opinions.
— BILL HOLM

The American Heritage Dictionary, fourth edition, defines
"liberal" in this way: "Favoring proposals for reform, open to
new ideas for progress, and tolerant of the ideas and behaviors
of others; broad-minded." I've always seen it as an ethos in
which possibility gets way out in front of reality
and takes a flying leap.
— ANNA QUINDLEN

We may be brothers after all. We will see.
— CHIEF SEATTLE

There's no growth without a lot of hard work and a little risk.
It's important to me that I continue to grow.
There's no point in living life any other way.
— GLORIA ESTEFAN

Many creative persons have benefited from mentors, role
models who guided them along the way to developing their
own uniqueness. And the creative mind also needs a degree of
solitude to match its immersion in the world, a time to mull
things over and get down to the work of composing,
painting, or writing alone.
— F. BARRON, A. MONTUORI, & A. BARRON

ELEVEN

The world is ruled by letting things take their course.

— *Lao Tzu*

Poverty is the mother of manhood.

— *Lucan*

Every time we suffer, we grow.

— *Ram Dass*

It is the duty of youth to bring fresh new powers to bear on social progress. Each generation of young people should be to the world like a vast reserve force to a tired army. They should move the world forward. That is what they are for.

— *Charlotte Perkins Gilman*

We do not understand ourselves yet and descend farther from heaven's air if we forget how much the natural world means to us. Signals abound that the loss of life's diversity endangers not just the body but the spirit. If that much is true, the changes occurring now will visit harm on all generations to come.

— *E. O. Wilson*

As we evolve as people, we must also enhance the way we educate our little ones. I know that mine are much smarter than me. I want to unlock their beautiful brains and expose those treasures.

— *Melanie Griffith*

While the U.S. is trying to figure out how to pay for its incursion into Iraq, millions of teenagers and young adults, especially in the inner cities, are drifting aimlessly from one day to the next. They're out of school, out of work, and all but out of hope.

— *Bob Herbert*

JASON A. MERCHEY

Moral philosophy was always the exercise of free, disciplined
reason alone. It was not based on religion, much less on
revelation, as civic religion was neither a guide nor a rival to it.
Its focus was the idea of the highest good as an attractive ideal,
as the reasonable pursuit of our true happiness...

— *JOHN RAWLS*

Because man and woman are the complement of one another,
we need woman's thought in national affairs to make a safe
and stable government.

— *ELIZABETH CADY STANTON*

Gilgamesh, where are you running?
You will not find the immortal life you seek.

— *UNKNOWN MESOPOTAMIAN AUTHOR*

In the end, I want to take many of the steps that people are
proposing: stopping the perpetrators and defending against
recurrences [of terrorism]. But I also want to look for, and
eliminate, the root causes, which will stop the pipeline from
being continually filled with soldiers ready to engage in
terrorism. And that's going to take a searching self-examination
of the behavior of our nation state.

— *ROBERT W. FULLER*

We can't make our kids care, we can't pour into them a social
conscience. But we can put before them prompts and
possibilities that will increase the odds. Our efforts won't be
perfect, and they won't always work, but we will have tried,
and that's all we can do. The rest is up to them.

— *SUSAN VOGT*

Transcendental intelligence rises when the intellectual mind
reaches its limit and if things are to be realized in their true
and essential nature, the process of thinking must be
transcended by an appeal to some higher faculty of cognition.

— *SIDDHARTHA GAUTAMA*

ELEVEN

This is no simple reform. It really is a revolution. Sex and race, because they are easy and visible differences, have been the primary ways of organizing human beings into superior and inferior groups and into the cheap labor on which this system still depends. We are talking about a society in which there will be no roles other than those chosen or those earned. We are really talking about humanism.

— GLORIA STEINEM

The devil loves nothing more than intolerance of reformers.

— JAMES RUSSELL LOWELL

For millennia of recorded history, the human spirit has been imprisoned by the fetters of androcracy [the dominator cultural model]. Our minds have been stunted, and our hearts have been numbed. And yet our striving for truth, beauty, and justice has never been extinguished. As we break out of these fetters, as our minds, hearts, and hands are freed, so also will be our creative imagination.

— RIANE EISLER

Human progress never rolls in on wheels of inevitability; it comes through the tireless efforts of men willing to be coworkers with God, and without this hard work, time itself becomes an ally of the forces of social stagnation.

— MARTIN LUTHER KING, JR.

Television is the best gauge we have of our decay.

— JAN STEVENSON

Current events and front page headlines have made us all aware of the importance of ethical conduct and personal integrity. In the wake of terrorist attacks, corporate scandals, and the betrayal of public trust, people are recognizing that duty, heroism, honesty, and self-respect are more valuable today than ever before. People are realizing that the twenty-first century needs a Code of Chivalry.

— SCOTT FARRELL

177

JASON A. MERCHEY

Can the Ethiopian change his skin, or the leopard his spots?
— *JEREMIAH 13:23*

Our love of what is beautiful does not lead to extravagance;
our love of things of the mind does not make us soft.
— *PERICLES*

...doing the best at this moment puts you in the best place
for the next moment.
— *OPRAH WINFREY*

I must emphasize that merely thinking that compassion and
reason and patience are good, will not be enough to develop
them. We must wait for difficulties to arise and then attempt to
practice these qualities. And who creates such opportunities?
Not our friends, of course, but our enemies.
— *TENZIN GYATSO*

When we recognize that we are dependent on other species –
the oxygen from the trees, the food that earthworms and
millions of soil organisms provide for us sustainably, our
paradigms shift to taking care of biodiversity instead of wiping
it out in the name of progress and development.
— *VANDANA SHIVA*

When white people and brown people and black people vote
together, that's when we make social progress in this country.
— *HOWARD DEAN*

The challenge now is to practice politics as the art of making
what appears to be impossible, possible.
— *HILLARY RODHAM CLINTON*

ELEVEN

If the concept of God has any validity or use, it can only be to
make us larger, freer, and more loving. If God cannot do this,
it is time we got rid of him.

— JAMES BALDWIN

One of the indictments of civilization is that happiness and
intelligence are so rarely found in the same person.

— WILLIAM FEATHER

People tend to spend their adult years either reliving or trying
to terminate the image they carried in high school.

— JASON MERCHEY

It is a spiritually impoverished nation that permits infants
and children to be the poorest Americans.

— MARIAN WRIGHT EDELMAN

With changes in education caused by the discovery of a world
consciousness, parochial leadership caught in the old ways of
imperialism, colonialism, and absolutism may change if people,
through social movements, de-legitimate warrior
and oppressor states.

— MARCUS G. RASKIN

The single most important strength a society can have
is a committed, reformist elite.

— FAREED ZAKARIA

If man is to be able to love, he must be put in his supreme
place. The economic machine must serve him, rather than he
serve it. Society must be organized in such a way that man's
social, loving nature is not separated from his social existence,
but becomes one with it.

— ERICH FROMM

JASON A. MERCHEY

Parents can give good advice or put them on the right track,
but the final forming of a person's character
lies in their own hands.

— *ANNE FRANK*

The way of the superior man is threefold, but I have not been
able to attain it. The man of wisdom has no perplexities; the
man of humanity has no worry; the man of courage has no fear.

— *CONFUCIUS*

Character calls forth character.

— *JOHANN WOLFGANG VON GOETHE*

I had once believed that we were all masters of our fate; that
we could mould our lives into any form we pleased... I had
overcome deafness and blindness sufficiently to be happy,
and I supposed that anyone could come out victorious if he
threw himself valiantly into life's struggle. But as I went more
and more about the country I learned that I had spoken with
assurance on a subject I knew little about. I forgot that I
owed my success partly to the advantages of my birth and
environment... Now, however, I learned that the power
to rise in the world is not within the reach of everyone.

— *HELEN KELLER*

Psychoanalysis is concerned with the past; while one is
analyzing the past one is missing the challenges of the present.

— *JIDDU KRISHNAMURTI*

The mark of the immature man is that he wants to die nobly
for a cause, while the mark of the mature man is he wants to
live humbly for one.

— *J. D. SALINGER*

ELEVEN

It's very important to me not to have my middle age be a
repeat of my youth, and my old age not to be a
repeat of my middle age.

— *Linda Ronstadt*

Give me the children until they are seven and
anyone may have them afterwards.

— *St. Francis Xavier*

Wisdom lies neither in fixity nor in change,
but in the dialectic between the two.

— *Octavio Paz*

Alas! How our enthusiasm decreases
as our experience increases!

— *Louise Colet*

Progress is life, standing still is death.

— *Pir-o-Murshid Hazrat Inayat Khan*

To be a human being means to possess a feeling of inferiority,
which constantly presses towards its own conquest...
The greater the feeling of inferiority that has been
experienced, the more powerful is the urge for conquest
and the more violent the emotional agitation.

— *Alfred Adler*

The person who tries to live alone will not succeed as a human
being. His heart withers if it does not answer another heart. His
mind shrinks away if he hears only the echoes of his own
thoughts and finds no other inspiration.

— *Pearl S. Buck*

JASON A. MERCHEY

Mothers of prejudiced children, far more than mothers of
unprejudiced children, held that obedience is the most
important thing a child can learn.

— *GORDON W. ALLPORT*

Why not learn by getting down to the actual practice?

— *MOHANDAS K. GANDHI*

What is the most beautiful in virile men is something feminine;
what is most beautiful in feminine women is something
masculine.

— *SUSAN SONTAG*

You've got to get people to believe that change is possible...
You have to show them that you can fight things successfully
even if you don't win.

— *WINONA LADUKE*

Much male fear of feminism is the fear that, in becoming whole
human beings, women will cease to mother men, to provide the
breast, the lullaby, the continuous attention associated by the
infant with the mother. Much male fear of feminism is
infantilism – the longing to remain the mother's son,
to possess a woman who exists purely for him.

— *ADRIENNE RICH*

To bring up a child the way he should go, travel that way
yourself once in a while.

— *JOSH BILLINGS*

I'm not sure that I was raised as much as I am raising myself.

— *AMBIKA TALWAR*

ELEVEN

The penalty for success is to be bored by the people
who used to snub you.

— *NANCY ASTOR*

Human nature is not a machine to be built after a model, and
set to do exactly the work prescribed for it, but a tree, which
requires to grow and develop itself on all sides, according to
the tendency of the inward forces which make it a living thing.

— *JOHN STUART MILL*

I expect to plead not for the slave only, but for suffering
humanity everywhere. Especially do I mean to labor for the
elevation of my sex.

— *LUCY STONE*

Decide what you want. Decide what you are willing to exchange
for it. Establish your priorities and go to work.

— *H. L. HUNT*

Just as the twig is bent, the tree is inclined.

— *ALEXANDER POPE*

He's got to make his own mistakes,
And learn to mend the mess he makes.
He's old enough to know what's right, but young enough
not to choose it.
He's noble enough to win the world, but weak
enough to lose it.
He's a New World Man…

— *NEIL PEART*

Only in growth, reform, and change, paradoxically enough, is
true security to be found.

— *ANNE MORROW LINDBERGH*

JASON A. MERCHEY

I know of no way of judging the future by the past.
— *PATRICK HENRY*

No life is so hard that you can't make it easier
by the way you take it.
— *ELLEN GLASGOW*

If you don't want to be average, don't do average things often.
— *JORDAN METZGER*

The art of writing is the art of discovering what you believe.
— *DAVID HARE*

As a Mexican, I always look to America as an example of what
freedom means. As a Jew, I always admired how this country
accepted and respected our traditions and beliefs. Now, as an
American citizen, I'm proud to be a part of a nation that stands
together, looking toward the future, with dignity and strength.
— *PEPE STEPENSKY*

The greatest challenge of the day is: how to bring about a
revolution of the heart, a revolution which has
to start with each one of us?
— *DOROTHY DAY*

Each needs to develop the sides of his personality
which he has neglected.
— *ALEXIS CARREL*

The past is not a package one can lay away.
— *EMILY DICKINSON*

ELEVEN

[The human being] is always in a dynamic self-actualizing process, always exploring, molding himself, and moving into the immediate future.

— *ROLLO MAY*

Too much focus on profit is no good; neither is too much social activism while ignoring profit. Capitalism for the common good, community action for economic strength – two sides of one coin. That's what nourishes me and my business.

— *JUDY WICKS*

Few men make themselves masters of the things they write or speak.

— *JOHN SELDEN*

Sometimes a person has to go back, really back – to have a sense, an understanding of all that's gone on to make them – before they can go forward.

— *PAULIE MARSHALL*

Don't judge each day by the harvest you reap, but by the seeds you plant.

— *ROBERT LOUIS STEVENSON*

Growing is the reward of learning.

— *MALCOLM X*

If we don't change, we don't grow. If we don't grow, we aren't really living.

— *GAIL SHEEHY*

Real progress and real reform won't happen without an understanding of the real truth.

— *BOB HERBERT*

JASON A. MERCHEY

It is easier to live through someone else than to become
complete yourself.
— *Betty Friedan*

Let the truth of Love be lighted,
Let the love of Truth shine clear,
Sensibility, armed with sense and liberty,
With the Heart and Mind united,
In a single, perfect sphere.
— *Neil Peart*

For human beings are not so constituted that they can live
without expansion; and if they do not get it one way,
they must another, or perish.
— *Margaret Fuller*

People cry much easier than they change.
— *James Baldwin*

Natural rights philosophy did not represent for Thomas
Jefferson, as it did for others, a learned discourse going back to
the Stoics. Rather, it delivered a warrant to dismantle the old
social order so that men (strictly speaking it was men, alas),
long alienated from their true natures, might recover them.
— *Joyce Appleby*

The highest possible stage in moral culture is when we
recognize that we ought to control our thoughts.
— *Charles Darwin*

You can lead a whore to culture, but you can't make her think.
— *Dorothy Parker*

ELEVEN

Progressive social movements do not simply produce statistics and narratives of oppression; rather, the best ones do what great poetry always does: transport us to another place, compel us to relive horrors, and more importantly, enable us to imagine a new society.

— *Robin D. G. Kelley*

In fact, I have a rather conservative attitude toward social change: since we're dealing with complex systems which nobody understands very much, the sensible move is to make changes and then see what happens – and if they work, make further changes.

— *Noam Chomsky*

The prime force behind ethical acts is not conscious choice, but rather deep-seated intuitions, predispositions, and habitual patterns of behavior related to our central identity.

— *Kristen Renwick Monroe*

To accomplish great things we must dream as well as act.

— *Anatole France*

In contrast to symbiotic union, mature love is union under the condition of preserving one's integrity, one's individuality. Love is an active power in man; a power which breaks through the walls which separate man from his fellow men, which unites him with others; love makes him overcome the sense of isolation and separateness, yet it permits him to be himself, to retain his integrity. In love, the paradox occurs that *two beings become one and yet remain two.*

— *Erich Fromm*

Judaism matters to the whole world because it is a system for making human beings decent, for turning men into menschen. The timeless mission of the Jews is to make the world better by making people better.

— *Jeff Jacoby*

JASON A. MERCHEY

Old-fashioned ways which no longer apply to changed
conditions are a snare in which the feet of women have always
become readily entangled.

— *JANE ADDAMS*

I've seen up close whom Congress responds to and who is left
out. We will never reorder the policy and priorities unless
we reorder the power.

— *PAUL WELLSTONE*

Prejudices, it is well known, are most difficult to eradicate from
the heart whose soil has never been loosened or fertilized by
education; they grow there, firm as weeds among rocks.

— *CHARLOTTE BRONTË*

If society will not admit of woman's free development,
then society must be remodeled.

— *ELIZABETH BLACKWELL*

How often the deepest convictions of one generation are
the rejects of the next.

— *LEARNED HAND*

Our development is set in motion from the moment of
conception. For example, does a child's mother use unsafe amounts and
types of drugs, or not? Are there high levels of stress hormones coursing
through her veins while a child is in utero? After birth we continue
growth at an incredible rate. Anyone who has watched an infant or young
child knows that learning and growing are fiercely fun. Still, our
development as a young child is somewhat outside of our control. Using
a metaphor to describe the process of growth, Alexander Pope put it,
"Just as the twig is bent, the tree's inclined," meaning that we grow up in
a certain way based on our environment. But, with this growth comes an
increasing responsibility for who we are and how we arrive at who we are.
Our development is also under the constraints of the systems in which we

ELEVEN

live, for example, during times of war a child is under duress. Our genes do set certain boundaries for us, but – and this is where the humanists and existentialists come in – the individual has some degree of opportunity and responsibility for progress. "I'm not sure that I was raised as much as I *am raising* myself" is how the artist and teacher Ambika Talwar spoke of the task of developing her potential. Life offers glorious possibilities: even in illness and dying we usually have choices regarding how and who we will be; for death is, as far as we know for sure, the final stage of human development.

CHAPTER TWELVE

PASSION, WILLINGNESS TO RISK, & SELF-AWARENESS

Self-awareness is knowing one's self, and willingness to feel and perceive what is going on inside. Emotion is another way of describing this virtue. Self-awareness can round out a person's repertoire of skills that, in some, is lopsided in favor of the intellectual and masculine. As illustration, how can a military strategist keep in mind the real-life consequences and repercussions of his battle planning? If he separates emotional facts from intellectual ones, is he not missing an important piece of the equation? Society can improve by including emotional facts in dry cost-benefit analyses – or not, such as the long time it has taken America to realize the need for passing anti-child-abuse legislation. On the other hand, emotions can get the better of a person, as in the case of police being too heavy-handed with suspects – in situations like this, self-awareness means controlling emotions. Consider the corporate decision maker who relocates jobs to another country, and in doing so, betrays the working class employees –making decisions without emotional understanding of how this affects people. If we were all more self-aware, then our empathy for others would have a much greater impact on our moral decision-making. This chapter seeks to deepen the human experience, which if checked by the thinking mind makes one's life more ethical – and more *worth living*.

Artificial manners vanish the moment
the natural passions are touched.

— MARIA EDGEWORTH

JASON A. MERCHEY

To be an artist it is necessary to live with our eyes wide open, to breathe in the colors of mountain and sky, to know the sound of leaves rustling, the smell of snow, the texture of bark. It is necessary to rub our hands all over life, to notice every beautiful and tragic thing, to cry freely, to collect experience and shape it into forms that others can share.

— *Jan Phillips*

I was sad to see my father cry, but I understood it, because sometimes a man has to cry.

— *Rudolfo A. Anaya*

To sing is to love and to affirm, to fly and soar, to coast into the hearts of the people who listen, to tell them that life is to live, that love is there, that nothing is a promise, but that beauty exists, and must be hunted for and found.

— *Joan Báez*

So you see, I grew up in a family that took for granted that one of life's greatest joys is engagement. We assumed that developing one's thinking in lively interchange in order to act responsibly is part of what it means to be fully alive.

— *Frances Moore Lappé*

When you are inspired by some great purpose, some extraordinary project, all your thoughts break their bounds: your mind transcends limitations, your consciousness expands in every direction, and you find yourself in a new, great, and wonderful world.

— *Patanjali*

TWELVE

Lest my way of life sound puritanical or austere, I always emphasize that in the long run one can't satisfactorily say no to war, violence, and injustice unless one is simultaneously saying yes to life, love, and laughter.

— *DAVID DELLINGER*

There is something about the present which we would not exchange, though we were offered a choice of all past ages to live in.

— *VIRGINIA WOOLF*

Falling in love is good! Just be careful not to fall so hard that you're knocked unconscious.

— *JASON MERCHEY*

They deem me mad because I will not sell my days for gold; and I deem them mad because they think my days have a price.

— *KAHLIL GIBRAN*

The facts of this world seen clearly are seen through tears.

— *MARGARET ATWOOD*

Little do men perceive what solitude is, and how far it extendeth. For a crowd is not company, and faces are but a gallery of pictures, and talk but a tinkling cymbal, where there is no love.

— *FRANCIS BACON*

When you only have two pennies left in the world, buy a loaf of bread with one, and a lily with the other.

— *CHINESE PROVERB*

JASON A. MERCHEY

As you are able to give energy to your passion, purpose will emerge. Clarity of purpose comes from honoring what gives your life meaning. Work has become devoid of meaning because people are asked to follow instructions rather than their creativity. True work is an expression of following our inner voice, heeding the spiritual call, and living your passion.
— *Justine Willis Toms & Michael Toms*

Happiness makes up in height what it lacks in length.
— *Robert Frost*

They sicken of the calm who know the storm.
— *Dorothy Parker*

There are two kinds of adventurers: those who go truly hoping to find adventure and those who go secretly hoping they won't.
— *Rabindranath Tagore*

For oft, when on my couch I lie
In vacant or in pensive mood,
They flash upon that inward eye
Which is the bliss of solitude;
And then my heart with pleasure fills,
And dances with the daffodils.
— *William Wordsworth*

Wild in the woods of love,
We harm those whom we adore;
And contrary to all good intentions,
We suffocate them in an alarming embrace.
— *Brendan Perry & Lisa Gerrard*

City life. Millions of people being lonely together.
— *Henry David Thoreau*

TWELVE

Kansas had better stop raising corn and begin raising hell.

— *MARY ELIZABETH LEASE*

They are not long, the weeping and the laughter, love and desire and hate. They are not long, the days of wine and roses.

— *ERNEST DOWSON*

In the days of Siddhartha Gautama, or in the days of Lao Tzu, the world was very very peaceful, natural, it was a heaven. Why? The population was very very small, one thing. People were not thinkers too much, they were more and more prone to feeling rather than thinking.

— *OSHO RAJNEESH*

Pity me that the heart is slow to learn
What the swift mind beholds at every turn.

— *EDNA ST. VINCENT MILLAY*

I keep going, of course. Otherwise I'd fade out.
And I don't intend to fade out, I intend to check out.

— *STUDS TERKEL*

I don't think of all the misery, but of the beauty that still remains. My advice is: Go outside, to the fields, enjoy nature and the sunshine, go out and try to recapture happiness in yourself and in God.

— *ANNE FRANK*

Either the soul is immortal and we live forever and we shall not die, or it perishes with the flesh, and we shall not know then that we are dead. Live, then, as if you were eternal.

— *ANDRE MAUROIS*

JASON A. MERCHEY

The bitterest tears shed over graves are for words left unsaid
and deeds left undone.

— *HARRIET BEECHER STOWE*

When we really begin to live in the world, then we understand
what is meant by brotherhood or mankind, and not before.

— *SRI SWAMI VIVEKANANDA*

My ideas usually come not at my desk writing,
but in the midst of living.

— *ANAIS NIN*

Temper is a quality that at a critical moment brings out
the best in steel and the worst in men.

— *WILLIAM P. GROHSE*

To the joyless man death is a blessing.

— *AFRICAN PROVERB*

The truest expression of a people is in its dances and its music;
bodies never lie.

— *AGNES DEMILLE*

The opposite of death is not life; it's indifference.

— *ELIE WIESEL*

The wild regrets and the bloody sweats none knew so well as I,
for he who lives more lives than one,
more deaths than one must die.

— *OSCAR WILDE*

Security is mostly an illusion. It does not exist in nature, nor
does humankind as a whole experience it. Avoiding danger is
no safer in the long run than outright exposure. Life is either a
daring adventure or nothing.

— *HELEN KELLER*

TWELVE

Now is the time to make real the promises of democracy,
now is the time...

— MARTIN LUTHER KING, JR.

Only a decade that put the lid on discourse as tightly as the '50s
did could have exploded into the free association of the '60s.

— ANNA QUINDLEN

My music is best understood by children and animals.

— IGOR STRAVINSKY

Until one has loved an animal,
a part of one's soul remains unawakened.

— ANATOLE FRANCE

You, whose day it is, make it beautiful.
Get out your rainbow colors, so it will be beautiful.

— NOOTKA SONG

Within our dreams and aspirations we find our opportunities.

— SUE ATCHLEY EBAUGH

Idle men are dead all their life long.

— ENGLISH PROVERB

What did my hands do before they held you?

— SYLVIA PLATH

Finally, though I have had to speak at some length about sex, I
want to make it as clear as I possibly can that the center of
Christian morality is not here. If anyone thinks that Christians
regard unchastity as the supreme vice, he is quite wrong. The
sins of the flesh are bad, but they are the least bad of all sins.

— C. S. LEWIS

JASON A. MERCHEY

Let our sleeping soul remember, and be awake and be alive,
in contemplation of how our life passes away, of how our death
comes forward to us, so silently.

— *Jorge Manrique*

Men's relationships are more like alliances.
They support one another, but always with wariness.

— *Anne Campbell*

Alas, I live an unexamined life.
Socrates would most certainly look upon me with contempt –
Though I may desire more excitement,
I oft' bow to inertia and fail to make any attempt.
We let sand pass through the hourglass as though it is limitless.

— *Jason Merchey*

Begin each day as if it were on purpose.

— *Mary Anne Radmacher*

I love my life; if not, it would not be worth dying for.

— *Chief Looking Glass*

Writing does not exclude the full life. It demands it.

— *Katherine Anne Porter*

Our scars have the power to remind us that the past was real.

— *Thomas Harris*

The best passion is compassion.

— *Jamaican proverb*

Don't end up saying, "If only…"

— *Katie Couric*

TWELVE

We who thirst for reason want to look our experiences in the
eye as severely as a scientific experiment...! We ourselves want
to be our experiments and guinea pigs.

— FRIEDRICH NIETZSCHE

While it is heartening to see young people excited about
learning and cognizant of the political implications of science,
it worries me when they believe that simply "droppin' science"
on the people will generate new, liberatory social movements.

— ROBIN D. G. KELLEY

What you need is sustained outrage...there's far too much
unthinking respect given to authority.

— MOLLY IVINS

Everyone knows they're going to die, but nobody believes it.
If we did, we would do things differently.

— MORRIE SCHWARTZ

There is a lot to be learned,
And you learn when your heart gets burned.

— MARTIN GORE

The only theology worth doing is that which inspires and
transforms lives, that which empowers us to participate in
creating, liberating, and blessing the world.

— CARTER HEYWARD

To a certain extent, we in Africa have always had a gift for
enjoying man for himself. It is at the heart of our traditional
culture, but now we see the possibility of extending the scale of
our discovery by example to the whole world. Let the West have
its technology and Asia its mysticism. Africa's gift to world
culture must be in the realm of human relationships!

— KENNETH KAUNDA

JASON A. MERCHEY

The soul should always stand ajar,
ready to welcome the ecstatic experience.

— EMILY DICKINSON

Instead of always thinking about our plans and anxiously
looking to the future, or giving ourselves up to regret for the
past, we should never forget that the present is the only reality,
the only certainty; the future almost always turns out contrary
to our expectations; the past, too, was very different from
what we suppose it to have been.

— ARTHUR SCHOPENHAUER

If facts are the seeds that later produce knowledge and wisdom,
then the emotions and the impressions of the senses are the
fertile soil in which the seeds must grow.

— RACHEL CARSON

Beauties in vain their pretty eyes may roll;
Charms strike the sight, but merit wins the soul.

— ALEXANDER POPE

Through all the tumult and the strife,
I hear its music ringing;
It sounds an echo in my soul.
How can I keep from singing?

— EITHNE NI BHRAONAIN

Writing is an artificial activity.
It is a lonely and private substitute for conversation.

— BROOKS ATKINSON

I have loved him too much not to feel any hatred for him.

— JEAN RACINE

TWELVE

The only way to live is to accept each minute as an unrepeated
miracle, which is exactly what it is – a miracle,
and unrepeatable.

— *Author Unknown*

For I am my mother's daughter, and the drums of Africa still
beat in my heart. They will not let me rest while there is a
single Negro boy or girl without a chance to prove his worth.

— *Mary McLeod Bethune*

We are always complaining that our days are few, and acting
as though there would be no end to them.

— *Seneca*

The butterfly counts not months, but moments,
and has time enough.

— *Rabindranath Tagore*

This sense of excitement, of devotion, and of patriotism
in the end prevailed.

— *Robert J. Oppenheimer*

We must do more to stop this senseless violence. We can't just
talk about it and then do nothing until the next shooting when
we will profess shock again. We must act now to get to the root
causes of the problem...

— *Marian Wright Edelman*

Any man who is attached to things of this world is one who
lives in ignorance and is being consumed by the snakes
of his own passions.

— *Black Elk*

It serves me right, for putting all my eggs in one bastard.

— *Dorothy Parker*

JASON A. MERCHEY

I never did a day's work in my life. It was all fun.
— THOMAS EDISON

Spend the afternoon. You can't take it with you.
— ANNIE DILLARD

If spring came but once in a century instead of once a year, or burst forth with the sound of an earthquake and not in silence, what wonder and expectation there would be in all hearts to behold the miraculous change.
— HENRY WADSWORTH LONGFELLOW

It takes a lot of courage to show your dreams to someone else.
— ERMA BOMBECK

I recently asked a wise man what I was to do now. He looked into my eyes, tilted his head slightly, and said, "Live."
— HOBI READER

Thoroughly living life requires initiative, risk taking, sustained action against the odds, making sacrifices for ideals and for others, and leaps of faith. People who live such lives report being happy, hopeful, and exhilarated – even when they fail.
— LAURA SCHLESINGER

You don't get much out of the passive consumption of pleasure, compared to enjoyment that is active, creative, and self-directive.
— MIHALY CSIKSZENTMIHALYI

The essence of romance is uncertainty.
— OSCAR WILDE

This incredible exchange of energy goes on onstage, where you're almost transported. For me, the spark comes – very emotional – from the shared experience of what I'm singing about. Or the band when we really lock it in and the audience knows you're locking in. I wish I could lose myself more when I play by myself. It's easy to do with an audience...

— BONNIE RAITT

I'm happy when life's good; when it's bad, I cry. I got values, but I don't know how or why.

— PETE TOWNSHEND

What happens to a dream deferred?
Does it dry up
Like a raisin in the sun...?
Or does it explode?

— LANGSTON HUGHES

We have to realize that we are as deeply afraid to live and to love as we are to die.

— R. D. LAING

As long as you can still be disappointed, you are still young.

— SARAH CHURCHILL

So much is at stake in the new year that despair is not an option. Better by far to heed the poet and double the heart's might.

— WILLIAM SLOANE COFFIN

Believe me, wise men don't say, "I shall live to do that." Tomorrow, life's too late. Live today.

— MARTIAL

JASON A. MERCHEY

We do not live long, the big and the small.
— *ANDRE THE GIANT*

There came a time when the risk to remain tight in the bud
was more painful than the risk it took to blossom.
— *ANAIS NIN*

When we avoid being vulnerable, we invest our
energy in defenses.
— *JACK SCHWARTZ*

...the oppressed have a right to class-hatred against the class
that is oppressing them.
— *ROBIN MORGAN*

Throw away your pitiful apathy and act boldly in this crisis!
A wise person shows energy and resolve; success is in her power,
no matter what.
— *SIDDHARTHA GAUTAMA*

It is hard to realize the gifts of people whom we do not know.
It is impossible to develop our gifts without a web of human
relationships. It is also harder to be kind. Because we don't
know the people with whom we are interacting, we can't
inquire about their problems or empathize with their troubles.
We don't notice they look stressed or tired. We can't
congratulate them on their children's victories. If we see social
interactions as the web that holds our lives in place, that web
is torn and tattered by the effects of our technology.
— *MARY PIPHER*

It doesn't have to be like this;
all we need to do is make sure we keep talking.
— *STEPHEN HAWKING*

TWELVE

Love is sacred, profound, joyous, and all that. Sex is…fun.
When the two come together, *the two come together.*

— *CHRISTIE BRINKLEY*

Wheresoever you go, go with all your heart.

— *CONFUCIUS*

Do human beings ever realize life while they live it?
– every, every minute?

— *THORNTON WILDER*

I received a certain Mexican passion not *for* life or *about* life,
but *in* life, a certain intensity in the daily living of it, a certain
abandon in…music, in the hugs, sometimes in the anger.

— *PAT MORA*

I have no idea of submitting tamely to injustice inflicted either
on me or on the slave. I will oppose it with all the moral powers
with which I am endowed. I am no advocate of passivity.

— *LUCRETIA MOTT*

Look to this day, for it is life. The very life of life. In its brief
course lay all the realities and verities of existence, the bliss of
growth, the splendor of action – the glory of power. For
yesterday is but a dream, and tomorrow is only a vision, but
today, well lived, makes every yesterday a dream of happiness
and every tomorrow a vision of hope.

— *SANSKRIT PROVERB*

Passion is like adding color to the otherwise black-and-white life.
Honor may be the act of looking at the panhandler in the eyes as you pass
by, but passion is buying him a meal after you do. I think most people live
a life that is, for the most part, missing passion. They go to work, they
interact with their spouse of seven years, they pay the bills. Life, especially
in our modern society, seems to sap the passion right out of us, such that

JASON A. MERCHEY

sex yields to fatigue and really talking with your significant other gives way to trite and superficial conversation. Passion is the difference between eating alone versus going out dancing. It is voting, it is taking a vacation, it is getting deeply enthralled in that reality-TV program. It is asking for a deserved raise, it is that hobby you lose yourself in, it is tickling your child until he can't take it anymore. Tell those in relationship to you what you really want to tell them, be willing to risk, open yourself up to feelings. Since I've got to live until my number is up, I might as well have as much color in my life as possible. "Only passions, great passions, can elevate the soul to great things" ~ Denis Diderot.

CHAPTER THIRTEEN

STRENGTH & COURAGE

Chivalry is something that I have always equated with courage and strength; images of cavalier men brandishing their swords to satisfy honor have fascinated me since I was young. And yet, in the modern world, strength and courage do not seem as attainable – or as valued – as they were during the Renaissance. Perhaps part of the problem is that in America, our leaders are known to "throw down gauntlets" and act dishonorably, and that we often seem to lack the strength to moderate ourselves – such as eating properly and exercising. I see that aggression in humankind is often the result of fear and cowardice rather than true courage or strength. Because of my experience in domestic violence intervention, I am quite aware of the way masculinity is mistaken for toughness and brutality. As a culture, we have a responsibility to promote the brands of courage that stay true to the highest meaning of the value. Many of the following quotations on courage and strength have a "motivational" feel; try writing some down and making a point of referring to them often. As of this writing, I have "Less Fear!" written in black marker on my bathroom mirror. It makes a difference!

More than bravado or bluster, today's knight in shining armor must have the courage of the heart necessary to undertake tasks which are difficult, tedious, or unglamorous, and to graciously accept the sacrifices involved.

— SCOTT FARRELL

JASON A. MERCHEY

My faith in the Constitution is whole, it is complete, it is total.
I am not going to sit here and be an idle spectator to the
diminution, the subversion, the destruction of the Constitution.

— BARBARA JORDAN

Most of us look at our ideals, say, how far we are from them,
and get depressed. But it is heroic simply to say, "Here are my
ideals," state them before the world, and then spend your life
trying to live up to them.

— KESHAVAN NAIR

Old age ain't no place for sissies.

— BETTE DAVIS

We will meet, all of us women of every land. We will meet at the
center and make a circle. We will weave a world web to
entangle the powers that bury our children.

— AUTHOR UNKNOWN

The problem is not hierarchy, but abuse of rank within it.

— ROBERT W. FULLER

Honest men may, and must, criticize America.

— W. E. B. DuBOIS

In these dangerous days, there is a right way and a wrong way
to be strong. Strength is more than tough words.

— JOHN F. KERRY

When I dare to be powerful – to use my strength in the service
of my vision – then it becomes less and less important
whether I am afraid.

— AUDRE LORDE

THIRTEEN

A woman is like a tea bag; you never know how strong
she is until she gets in hot water.

— *ELEANOR ROOSEVELT*

Communism is a hammer which we use to crush the enemy.

— *MAO ZEDONG*

Men say we [women] are ever cruel to each other. Let us end
this ignoble record and henceforth stand by womanhood.
If Victoria Woodhull must be crucified, let men drive the
spikes and plait the crown of thorns.

— *ELIZABETH CADY STANTON*

I do not wish to treat friendships daintily, but with the roughest
courage. When they are real, they are not glass thread or
frostwork, but the solidest thing we know.

— *RALPH WALDO EMERSON*

The darkness has a hunger that's insatiable. And the lightness
has a call that's hard to hear. So I wrap my fear around me like
a blanket; I sail my ship of safety until I sank it.

— *EMILY SALIERS & AMY RAY*

A leader or a man of action in a crisis almost always acts
subconsciously and then thinks of the reasons for his actions.

— *JAWAHARLAL NEHRU*

He who reaches for the stars must be willing to pay the cost.

— *MEXICAN PROVERB*

You can listen to what everybody says, but the fact remains that
you've got to get out there and do the thing yourself.

— *JOAN SUTHERLAND*

JASON A. MERCHEY

Every man who is truly a man must learn to be alone in the midst of all the others, and if need be against all the others.
— *ROMAIN ROLLAND*

Courage is the most important of all the virtues, because without it we can't practice any other virtue with consistency.
— *MAYA ANGELOU*

If we take the generally accepted definition of bravery as a quality when one knows not fear, I have never seen a brave man. All men are frightened. The more intelligent they are, the more they are frightened. The courageous man is the man who forces himself, in spite of his fear, to carry on. Discipline, pride, self-respect, self-confidence, and the love of glory are attributes which will make a man courageous even when he is afraid.
— *GEORGE S. PATTON, JR.*

Fall seven times, stand up eight.
— *JAPANESE PROVERB*

One of the greatest contributors to that so-called "fatal" mentality that is a part of me is the notion that, if I am called to duty and fail to act when I ought to have, what good is my life? How many times can one forgo opportunities to uphold one's cherished beliefs and still have a self-image as a "good" person?
— *JASON MERCHEY*

I am glad to see that men are getting their rights, but I want women to get theirs, and while the water is stirring I will step into the pool.
— *SOJOURNER TRUTH*

A clay pot sitting in the sun will always be a clay pot. It has to go through the white heat of a furnace to become porcelain.
— *MILDRED WITTE STRUVEN*

THIRTEEN

A man can stand a lot as long as he can stand himself. He can live without hope, without friends, without books, even without music, as long as he can listen to his own thoughts.

— *Axel Munthe*

Well-behaved women rarely make history.

— *Laurel Thatcher Ulrich*

The lonely one offers his hand too quickly to whomever he encounters.

— *Friedrich Nietzsche*

Courage! I have shown it for years; think you I shall lose it at the moment when my sufferings are about to end?

— *Marie Antoinette*

War is an unmitigated evil. But it certainly does one thing: It drives away fear and brings bravery to the surface.

— *Mohandas K. Gandhi*

When you appeal to force, there is one thing you must never do – lose.

— *Dwight D. Eisenhower*

Nobody can give you freedom. Nobody can give you equality or justice or anything. If you're a man, you take it.

— *Malcolm X*

In love there are no vacations... No such thing. Love has to be lived fully with its boredom and all that.

— *Marguerite Duras*

It takes courage to face and fight life; it takes great courage to end it.

— *John A. Marshall*

JASON A. MERCHEY

One must raise the self by the self
And not let the self sink down,
For the self's only friend is the self
And the self is the self's one enemy.
— *The Bhagavad-Gita*

Resistance to tyrants is obedience to God.
— *Thomas Jefferson*

Life shrinks or expands in proportion to one's courage.
— *Anais Nin*

Lisa Beamer, the widow of American patriot Todd Beamer, who
died attacking the would-be destroyers of the White House on
Flight 93 on 9-11-2001, subsequently found this quote of Teddy
Roosevelt while going through Todd's desk: "The credit
belongs to the man who is actually in the arena...who strives
valiantly, who knows the great enthusiasms, the great devotions,
and spends himself in worthy causes. Who, at best, knows the
triumph of high achievement and who, at worst, if he fails, fails
while daring greatly so that his place shall never be with those
cold and timid souls who know neither victory nor defeat."

In morals, what begins in fear usually ends in wickedness; in
religion, what begins in fear usually ends in fanaticism. Fear,
either as a principle or a motive, is the beginning of all evil.
— *Anna Jameson*

A good soldier is not violent. A good fighter is not angry.
— *Lao Tzu*

Pain nourishes courage. You can't be brave if you've only
had good things happen to you.
— *Mary Tyler Moore*

THIRTEEN

We all take different paths in life, but no matter where we go,
we take a little of each other everywhere.

— *TIM MCGRAW*

Tenderness and kindness are not signs of weakness and despair,
but manifestations of strength and resolutions.

— *KAHLIL GIBRAN*

You can't shake hands with a clenched fist.

— *INDIRA GANDHI*

Sometimes I think we're alone. Sometimes I think we're not. In
either case, the thought is staggering.

— *BUCKMINSTER FULLER*

If you can't bite, don't show your teeth.

— *YIDDISH PROVERB*

We won't believe the world can change until we experience
ourselves changing. There's only one way to change yourself:
risk…We have to risk being wrong,
and we have to risk being lonely.

— *FRANCES MOORE LAPPÉ*

If you don't want to be criticized, don't say anything,
do anything, or be anything.

— *ANONYMOUS*

Eternal are the heavens and the earth;
Old people are poorly off.
Do not be afraid.

— *CROW WARRIOR SONG*

To see what is right and not to do it is want of courage.

— *CONFUCIUS*

Your heart is a muscle the size of your fist:
keep loving, keep fighting.
— DALIA SAPON-SHEVIN

He has half the deed done who has made a beginning.
— HORACE

Faith is not trying to believe something regardless of the
evidence; faith is daring to do something regardless
of the consequences.
— SHERWOOD EDDY

It is easy enough to be pleasant,
When life flows by like a song,
But the man worthwhile is one who will smile,
When everything goes dead wrong.
— ELLA WHEELER WILCOX

Donald Rumsfeld often quotes Al Capone.
But should our guiding philosophy really be the
street talk of a Chicago mobster?
— FAREED ZAKARIA

Toughness doesn't have to come in a pinstripe suit.
— DIANNE FEINSTEIN

The darkest hour has only 60 minutes.
— MORRIS MANDEL

I don't think it's cowardly to be extremely wary of war,
especially "pre-emptive" war.
— KATHA POLLITT

Be bold, and mighty forces will come to your aid.
— JOHANN WOLFGANG VON GOETHE

THIRTEEN

If there is anybody in this land who thoroughly believes that the
meek shall inherit the earth, they have not often let their
presence be known.

— *W. E. B. DuBois*

Courage gives vibrancy to our values.

— *Laura Schlesinger*

If I should die, think this only of me:
That there's some corner of a foreign field
That is forever England.

— *Rupert Brooke*

No coward soul is mine,
No trembler in the world's storm-troubled sphere;
I see Heaven's glories shine,
And faith shines equal, arming me from fear.

— *Emily Brontë*

Courtesy is compatible with bravery.

— *Mexican proverb*

The three hardest tasks in the world are neither physical feats
nor intellectual accomplishments, but moral acts: to return love
for hate, to include the excluded, and to say, "I was wrong."

— *Sydney J. Harris*

We do not pray not to be tempted, but not to be conquered
when we are tempted.

— *Origines Adamantius*

To me, there is no greater act of courage than to be the
one who kisses first.

— *Janeane Garofalo*

Perfect valor is to do without witnesses what one would do
before all the world.
— FRANCOIS, DUC DE LA ROCHEFOUCAULD

It doesn't interest me who you are, how you came to be here.
I want to know if you will stand in the center of the fire with me
and not shrink back.
— ORIAH MOUNTAIN DREAMER

The danger in having enormous power is that the ambition to
use it for good can so often be subverted by the temptation
to use it for dominance.
— ANNA QUINDLEN

Demons strike the timid.
— TAMIL PROVERB

God may pardon you, but I never can.
— ELIZABETH I

To the bold man fortune gives her hand.
— SPANISH PROVERB

Don't be afraid if things seem difficult in the beginning.
That's only the initial impression. The important thing is
not to retreat; you have to master yourself.
— OLGA KORBUT

Adversity causes some men to break, others to break records.
— WILLIAM A. WARD

The conservative who resists change is as valuable
as the radical who proposes it.
— WILL & ARIEL DURANT

THIRTEEN

Death against one's will is that of ignorant men...
death with one's will is that of wise men.

— *THE JAINA SUTRAS*

Parents learn a lot from their children about coping with life.

— *MURIEL SPARK*

That in my troubled season I can cry
Upon the wide composure of the sky,
And envy fields, and wish that I might be
As little daunted as a star or tree.

— *JOHN DRINKWATER*

From Truman to Kennedy to Carter to Clinton, America has
contained, appeased, and retreated, often sacrificing America's
best interests and security.

— *ANN COULTER*

Today is a good day to die.

— *CHIEF CRAZY HORSE*

A wounded deer leaps highest.

— *EMILY DICKINSON*

It is the character of a brave and resolute man not to
be ruffled by adversity and not to desert his post.

— *CICERO*

To look life in the face, always to look life in the face, and to
know what it is, to love it for what it is. At last, to know it. To
love it for what it is. And then to put it away.

— *VIRGINIA WOOLF*

It is not a sin to have possessions –
but it is a sin for possessions to have us.

— *H. A. SCOGGINS*

JASON A. MERCHEY

Children who are closer to their birth, and thus to the
experience of oneness, rightly reject hypocrisy.
— *VIMALIA MCCLURE*

Where today are the Pequot? Where are the Narragansett, the
Mohican, the Pokanoket, and many other once powerful tribes
of our people? They have vanished before the avarice and the
oppression of the White Man, as snow before a summer sun.
Will we let ourselves be destroyed in our turn without a
struggle, give up our homes, our country bequeathed to us by
the Great Spirit, the graves of our dead and everything that is
dear and sacred to us? I know you will cry with me,
"Never! Never!"
— *CHIEF TECUMSEH*

Real courage is when you know you're licked before you begin,
but you begin anyway and see it through no matter what.
— *HARPER LEE*

What lies behind us and what lies before us are small matters
compared to what lies within us.
— *RALPH WALDO EMERSON*

Obedience is not enough. Power is inflicting pain and
humiliation, otherwise you cannot be sure. Power is tearing
human lives apart and putting them together again in new
shapes of your own choosing. Power is not a means,
it is an end.
— *GEORGE ORWELL*

[I went to Iraq during the second war to act as a human shield
because] I wanted to stand beside and protect those who were
caught between their domestic tyrant and U.S. ambitions.
I went in the hopes of stopping what I perceive as an
illegal and unnecessary war.
— *FAITH FIPPINGER*

THIRTEEN

On the day of victory, no fatigue is felt.

— *EGYPTIAN PROVERB*

Semi-educated people join cults whose whole purpose is to dull the pain of thought or take medications that claim to abolish anxiety. Oriental religions, with their emphasis on Nirvana and fatalism, are prepackaged for Westerners as therapy and platitudes or tautologies masquerade as wisdom.

— *CHRISTOPHER HITCHENS*

For millennia men have fought wars and the Blade has been a male symbol. But this does not mean men are violent and warlike. Throughout recorded history there have been peaceful and nonviolent men. Moreover, obviously there were both men and women in prehistoric societies where the power to give and nurture, which a Chalice symbolizes, was supreme. The underlying problem is not men as a sex. The root of the problem lies in a social system in which the power of the Blade is idealized – in which both men and women are taught to equate true masculinity with violence and to see men who do not conform to this ideal as "too soft" or "effeminate."

— *RIANE EISLER*

If you can't stand the heat, get out of the kitchen.

— *HARRY VAUGHAN*

The United States has waged war against Al Qaeda for two years, destroyed its home base, rolled up dozens of its cells, and shut down hundreds of bank accounts around the world. Yet it could not – and probably cannot – stop attacks on civilians. There are simply too many soft targets in the world. We've been tough on terror. It's time to get tough on the causes of terror.

— *FAREED ZAKARIA*

There is little place in the political scheme of things for
an independent, creative personality; for a fighter.
Anyone who takes that role must pay a price.
— *SHIRLEY CHISHOLM*

If a way to the Better there be, it exacts a full look at the Worst.
— *THOMAS HARDY*

We rely upon the poets, the philosophers, and the playwrights
to articulate what most of us can only feel, in joy or sorrow.
They illuminate the thoughts for which we only grope; they
give us the strength and balm we cannot find in ourselves.
Whenever I feel my courage wavering, I rush to them.
They give me the wisdom of acceptance, the will
and resilience to push on.
— *HELEN HAYES*

Trust, but be careful in whom.
— *ROMAN PROVERB*

Get place and wealth if possible, with grace;
If not, by any means, get wealth and place.
— *ALEXANDER POPE*

No matter what the fight, don't be ladylike! God almighty made
women and the Rockefeller gang of thieves made the ladies.
— *MARY JONES*

The news is going to get worse before it gets better.
The American people must be prepared for it and they
must get it straight from the shoulder.
— *FRANKLIN D. ROOSEVELT*

Boldly ventured is half won.
— *GERMAN PROVERB*

THIRTEEN

Gentleness sometimes doesn't sound strong. But you have
to have a strong personality and strong determination
to be gentle.

— *Kaicho Nakamura*

Do the thing you fear, and death of fear is certain.

— *Ralph Waldo Emerson*

If you ask a boy what strength is, you will hear that it involves physical prowess, domination, or superiority. But many, perhaps especially mothers, believe strength to be less an outward phenomenon and more of an internal state. Strength is allied to courage as well as integrity and dedication, but the wise can see the slight differences. Friedrich Nietzsche, a man who studied strength, recognized its many facets: "Independence is for the very few; it is a privilege of the strong." When one is in the minority, it takes strength to persevere. I think of the time when brave Americans charged the cockpit of the hijacked plane to fight blade-wielding terrorists, bringing it down into the woods and sparing the intended target. It is strong when a judge metes out justice despite the sobbing pleas from the nervous convict or political pressure. Another important characteristic of strength is how others surrounding the strong are treated: "I learned that it is the weak who are cruel, and that gentleness is to be expected only from the strong" ~ Leo Rosten.

CHAPTER FOURTEEN

TRUTH & JUSTICE

What does it mean to be just? Do we ever get our hands on truth, or is it impossible to do so? How fair is the world, and what can be done to increase the level of justice at home and in our society? What are some impediments to living a truthful life? The quotations included in this chapter attempt to provide "grist for the mill" about such profound questions as these. Since philosophy often does better at clarifying the big questions than it does providing solid answers to them, this chapter will be a challenge – but a challenge that can be met with the help of the wisdom contained in this final chapter. It is far easier to say that truth *always has been and always will be* so than it is to decide what is true. Some truths can be found within us, yet others require critical thought and objective information. However, it is important to remember that just because someone has more status, education, or charisma, it does not necessarily mean he or she has a better understanding *of* or a commitment *to* truth. Take young children, for example; because they have not yet grasped an understanding of social conventions, they simply tell it – or shout it – like it is (at times much to the irritation of any adults within earshot). Like you, I imagine, I am still trying to discover what is true and what isn't. Although science provides us with answers to some questions, it cannot be very helpful for other mysteries. And though our feelings may sometimes bring us closer to the truth, they may lead us astray as well. Thus, the road to truth and justice may be a very long one indeed.

In the fusion of two contradictory opinions shines the truth.　　223

— Anita Vélez-Mitchell

JASON A. MERCHEY

When we feel strongly about an issue, it is tempting to assume
that we just know what the truth must be, without even having
to consider the arguments on the other side. Unfortunately,
however, we cannot rely on our feelings, no matter how
powerful they may be.

— *James Rachels*

A democracy cannot flourish half rich and half poor, any more
than it can flourish half free and half slave.

— *Felix G. Rohatyn*

I have always preferred the agony of losing a certain destiny in
order to find my true self. Shipwrecked in a hollow,
unauthentic world, I prefer to advance staggeringly toward the
authenticity of life, even though it might lead me only toward
the authenticity of my own death.

— *Arturo Arias*

The arm of the moral universe is long, but it bends
toward justice.

— *Martin Luther King, Jr.*

I tore myself away from the safe comfort of certainties through
my love for truth; and truth rewarded me.

— *Simone de Beauvoir*

Formerly, when religion was strong and science weak, men
mistook magic for medicine; now, when science is strong and
religion weak, men mistake medicine for magic.

— *Thomas Szasz*

What does your anxiety do? It does not empty tomorrow of its
sorrow; but oh! it empties today of its strength.

— *Jan Maclaren*

FOURTEEN

Time, space, and causation are like the glass through which the Absolute is seen… In the Absolute there is neither time, space, nor causation.

— SRI SWAMI VIVEKANANDA

Law and justice are not always the same. When they aren't, destroying the law may be the first step toward changing it.

— GLORIA STEINEM

Saints should always be judged guilty until they are proven innocent.

— GEORGE ORWELL

Appearances are not held to be a clue to the truth. But we seem to have no other.

— IVY COMPTON-BURNETT

A warrior I have been. Now it is all over. A hard time I have.

— SITTING BULL

What does the thoughtful person do with the fact that there are no perfect examples of virtue? The man who harms the child molester while they are both in prison is injuring nevertheless. Woodrow Wilson was a racist. Our war with Iraq was as self-serving as it was liberating. Mother Teresa's image cracks under criticism. How many presidents were adulterers? We ought to study and extol the principle, not the person; people are by definition imperfect, whereas principles are, by definition, perfection.

— JASON MERCHEY

If the right to accumulate property is not constrained by the duty of *distributive justice,* the gap between the haves and the have-nots will become greater and greater.

— JUDITH A. BOSS

JASON A. MERCHEY

It is not truth that makes man great,
but man who makes truth great.
— CONFUCIUS

It is vital that people be presented with the truth. Today more
than ever we need what Einstein referred to as
"a chain reaction of awareness."
— HELEN CALDICOTT

If you speak the truth, have one foot in the stirrup.
— TURKISH PROVERB

Say not, "I have found the truth," but rather,
"I have found a truth."
— KAHLIL GIBRAN

We will work with the United Nations when we can,
and act unilaterally when we must.
— MADELEINE ALBRIGHT

Every government has a need to frighten its population, and
one way of doing that is to shroud its workings in mystery.
…That's the standard way you cloak and protect power: you
make it look mysterious and secret, above the ordinary person
– otherwise why should anybody accept it?
— NOAM CHOMSKY

A liberal is a conservative who's been arrested.
A conservative is a liberal who's been mugged.
— WENDY KAMINER

If any harm follows, then thou shalt give life for life, eye for eye,
tooth for tooth, hand for hand, foot for foot, burning for
burning, wound for wound, stripe for stripe.
— EXODUS 21:23-25

FOURTEEN

When one conception of God has ceased to have meaning or relevance, it has been quietly discarded and replaced by a new theology. A fundamentalist would deny this, since fundamentalism is antihistorical: it believes that Abraham, Moses, and the later prophets all experienced their God in exactly the same way as people do today. Yet if we look at our three religions, it becomes clear that there is no objective view of "God": each generation has to create the image of God that works for it.

— *Karen Armstrong*

We will never win as long as we allow ourselves to doubt that justice exists only when people are willing to defend it... May the lesson nourish the wisdom of resistance deep within our hearts.

— *Cecilia Rodríguez*

The superior man is ashamed if his words are better than his deeds.

— *Confucius*

Words may show a man's wit, but actions, his meaning.

— *Benjamin Franklin*

One of the tools for perpetuating oppression is the "tyranny of the majority," when 51 percent vote one way and 49 percent vote the other, and the 51 percent take home all the toys. It expedites process, but does not render justice.

— *Betty Burkes*

An independent reality in the ordinary physical sense can neither be ascribed to the phenomenon nor to the agencies of observation.

— *Niels Bohr*

JASON A. MERCHEY

The time of pretending that radicalism does not exist in Saudi Arabia is long past. How can we expect others to believe that a majority of us are a peace-loving people who denounce extremism and terrorism when some preachers continue to call for the destruction of Jews and Christians, blaming them for all the misery in the Islamic world?

— *RAID QUSTI*

If particular care and attention is not paid to the ladies, we are determined to foment a rebellion, and will not hold ourselves bound by any laws in which we have no voice or representation.

— *ABIGAIL ADAMS*

You know who were the worst traitors in the history of our country? The Confederates. They took up arms against soldiers wearing the uniform of the United States of America. But they were much, much worse than John Walker Lindh. Because they killed hundreds of thousands of American troops. And for what cause? So they could whip and torture black people. Why would anyone want to put up a flag honoring that?

— *AL FRANKEN*

Perhaps the biggest myth is that communication – and more specifically, learning to resolve your conflicts – is the royal road to romance and an enduring, happy marriage.

— *JOHN GOTTMAN & NAN SILVER*

The unique value of dreams for our waking life rests on the fact that we do something asleep and dreaming that we cannot do as well while awake. We look at ourselves with greater honesty and greater depth.

— *MONTAGUE ULLMAN*

Any religion which sacrifices women to the brutality of men is no religion....

— *JULIA WARD HOWE*

FOURTEEN

The hungry judge has soon the sentence signed,
And wretches hang – the jurymen may dine.
— *ALEXANDER POPE*

Glaciers [melting, due to global warming] don't give a damn
about politics – they just reflect reality.
— *AL GORE*

Those Americans who drew the short straw and live in poverty
are systematically shut out of the blessing of American society,
Horatio Alger success stories notwithstanding. Talk is cheap in
Washington, and talk about "values" is cheaper still. If we really
valued work, then the janitors and garbage collectors and
sweatshop workers and the rest of the hardworking poor would
be able to put food on the table. If we really valued children,
we'd make sure that the poorest of our children weren't taught
in hallways and broom closets or in shifts and we'd guarantee
that they all had textbooks and qualified, well-paid teachers.
— *NYDIA M. VELÁZQUEZ*

Truth can never be told so as to be understood,
and not believ'd.
— *WILLIAM BLAKE*

Literature, fiction, poetry – whatever – makes justice in the
world. That is why it almost always has to be on the side
of the underdog.
— *GRACE PALEY*

I established law and justice in the land.
— *HAMMURABI*

Useless laws weaken the necessary laws.
— *BARON DE MONTESQUIEU*

There is nothing to fear except the persistent refusal to find out the truth, the persistent refusal to analyze the causes of happenings.

— DOROTHY THOMPSON

Surely we do not need *human nature* to explain war; there are other explanations. But human nature is simple and easy. It requires very little thought. To analyze the social, economic, and cultural factors that throughout human history have led to so many wars – that is hard work.

— HOWARD ZINN

The greater tenacity of life among women, their greater resistance to disease, their larger capacity for continual, sustained effort...are ample proofs that women need not be invalids or "weak," and that it is a social mistake or a social crime, or both, if they are so in any prevailing numbers at any period of life.

— ANNA GARLIN SPENCER

Although no two Middle Eastern countries have identical l egal-religious systems, women are second-class citizens in all of them.

— AZAM KAMGUIAN

The average person's consciousness is mainly "false consciousness," consisting of fictions and illusion, while precisely what he is not aware of is *reality*.

— ERICH FROMM

Justice of right is always to take precedence over might.

— BARBARA JORDAN

In quarreling, the truth is always lost.

— PUBLILIUS SYRUS

FOURTEEN

Justice is better than chivalry if we cannot have both.

— *ALICE STONE BLACKWELL*

The truth often sounds paradoxical.

— *LAO TZU*

If what I do proves well, it won't advance,
They'll say it's stolen, or else it was by chance.

— *ANNE BRADSTREET*

Every day that we wake up is a good day. Every breath that we
take is filled with hope for a better day. Every word that we
speak is a chance to change what is bad into something good.
We aren't slaves... This nation is at least a *potential* democracy.
We need to wake up from this walking nightmare and realize
that the sun is shining.

— *WALTER MOSLEY*

The ultimate aim of the human mind, in all its efforts,
is to become acquainted with Truth.

— *ELIZA FARNHAM*

The just path is always the right one.

— *YIDDISH PROVERB*

You can't ignore politics, no matter how much you'd like to.

— *MOLLY IVINS*

To show that a given decision conflicts with what a principle
would dictate is to give a reason for thinking it is unjust.

— *JOHN RAWLS*

Being under illusion means perceiving objective appearances
and mental appearances as having independent reality.

— *BOKAR RINPOCHE*

JASON A. MERCHEY

It seemed to me certain, and I still think so today, that one can never wrestle enough with God if one does so out of pure regard for the truth. Christ likes us to prefer truth to him because, before being Christ, he is truth. If one turns aside from him to go toward the truth, one will not go far before falling into his arms.

— *SIMONE WEIL*

Socialism collapsed because it did not allow the market to tell the economic truth. Capitalism may collapse because it does not allow the market to tell the ecological truth.

— *OYSTEIN DAHLE*

John Adams, one of the American Revolution's most devoted patriots, was the lawyer who successfully defended the British captain and eight soldiers who had been charged with murder after the Boston Massacre of 1770. Although Adams was staunchly anti-British, and Boston was loudly clamoring for the execution of the soldiers, his belief in justice led him to accept their defense. He expected the action to end his career, but instead, it won the respect of his peers. And mine today.

— *ISAAC ASIMOV*

Poor human nature, what horrible crimes have been committed in thy name! Every fool, from king to policeman, from the flathead parson to the visionless dabbler in science, presume to speak authoritatively of human nature. The greater the mental charlatan, the more definite his insistence on the wickedness and weakness of human nature.

— *EMMA GOLDMAN*

All of the land, all of the forests and natural resources that have been stripped from their rightful owners will be immediately restored to the villages or citizens to whom they legally belong...

— *EMILIANO ZAPATA*

232

FOURTEEN

I see poetry as the courageous act of articulating reality.

— *DAVID WHYTE*

The real purpose of politics is to guarantee the rights and life
of the oppressed and the poor and help them to become the
principals of politics.

— *KIM DAE JUNG*

While it is true that our society must debate such controversial
issues as capital punishment, assisted suicide, and the like, we
must not forget that there exists a core of uncontroversial
ethical issues that were settled a long time ago.

— *CHRISTINA HOFF SUMMERS*

Cheating thrives where unfairness reigns, along with economic
anxiety. It thrives where government is the weak captive of
wealthy interests and lacks the will to do justice impartially.
It thrives where money and success are king, and winners are
fawned over whatever their daily abuses of power.

— *DAVID CALLAHAN*

You're not to be so blind with patriotism that you can't face
reality. Wrong is wrong, no matter who says or does it.

— *MALCOLM X*

Every time I close the door on reality, it comes in
through the windows.

— *JENNIFER UNLIMITED*

Don't confuse caring for weakness;
You can't put that label on me.
The truth is my weapon of mass protection
And I believe truth sets you free.

— *WILLIE NELSON*

Why should people feel aggrieved that the rich are pulling
further ahead if they are also moving forward?

— DINESH D'SOUZA

We live in a fantasy world, a world of illusion.
The great task in life is to find reality.

— IRIS MURDOCH

Democracy is the art of running the circus
from the monkey cage.

— H. L. MENCKEN

What is hard on criminals is to insist that they be accountable,
that they work hard, that they give back.

— MIMI SILBERT

Man knows that the world is not made on a human scale –
and he wishes it were.

— ANDRE MALRAUX

It may be necessary temporarily to accept a lesser evil,
but one must never label a necessary evil as good.

— MARGARET MEAD

The President is right – in many ways, we are a shining city on a
hill. But the hard truth is that not everyone is sharing in this
city's splendor and glory.

— MARIO CUOMO

Not by silence (alone) does he who is dull and ignorant
become a sage; but that wise man who, as if holding a pair of
scales, embraces the best and shuns evil, is indeed a sage.

— SIDDHARTHA GAUTAMA

If decade after decade the truth cannot be told…one's fellow
countrymen become harder to understand than Martians.

— ALEXANDER SOLZHENITSYN

FOURTEEN

The power I exert on the court depends on the power of my arguments, not on my gender.

— SANDRA DAY O'CONNOR

My atheism, like that of Spinoza, is true piety towards the universe and denies only gods fashioned by men in their own image, to be servants of their human interests.

— GEORGE SANTYANA

There remains a chasm between truth and reality. And the crucial question which confronts us in psychology and other aspects of the science of man is precisely this chasm between what is *abstractly true* and what is *existentially real* for the given living person.

— ROLLO MAY

It is absurd to suggest that students who attend the poorest schools have anywhere close to the same preparation and readiness as students who attend the wealthiest schools. People talk about using tests to motivate students to do well and to ensure that we close the achievement gap. But we cannot close the achievement gap until we close the gap in investments between rich and poor schools.

— PAUL WELLSTONE

Our fathers gave us many laws, which they have learned from their fathers; these laws were good. They told us to treat all men as they treated us; that we should never break a bargain; that it was a disgrace to tell a lie, that we should speak only the truth; that it was a shame for one man to take from another his wife, or his property without paying for it. We were taught to believe that the Great Spirit sees and hears everything and that He never forgets; that hereafter He will give every man a spirit home according to his desserts – if he has been a good man, he will have a good home; if he was bad, he will have a bad home. This I believe, and all my people believe the same.

— CHIEF JOSEPH

In my eyes, both Adolf Hitler and my grandfather were false
prophets of the twentieth century.
— SOPHIE FREUD

African-Americans have been on the lowest rung of the
economic ladder since the day they were beaten and dragged
here in chains – and they have *never made it off* that rung,
not for a single day.
— MICHAEL MOORE

There is no country in the world where there is so much
boasting of the "chivalrous" treatment she enjoys…In short,
indulgence is given her as a substitute for justice.
— HARRIET MARTINEAU

We're half the people; we should be half the Congress.
— JEANNETTE RANKIN

We want the truth. The President wants it. I want it. And the
American people have a fundamental right to it. And if the
truth hurts, so be it. We gotta take our lumps and move ahead.
— GEORGE H. W. BUSH

The existence of individual private property is responsible for
the immense inequalities of wealth and income in the world
today. Small numbers of individuals hold large amounts of
property, whether it takes the form of land, factories, mines, or
intellectual ideas. Billions, on the other hand, possess no
property of any sort and are forced to subsist on wages earned
in the market for labor, which in the last century has
increasingly turned against them.
— PRASANNAN PARTHASARATHI

It is not a question of how skillfully we play our cards but
of whether we were given a fair deck.
— BARRY SCHECK

FOURTEEN

Scientists from many universities, think tanks, NASA, the National Academy of Science, and the Association for the Advancement of Science are warning of planetary catastrophes that stem, at least in part, from unfettered economic expansion. Yet for the most part, these scientific prophets are ignored. If they are even half right, the system needs radical transformation, from the household level to the global economy. For now, the power brokers cannot accept this, and choose denial over truth.

— *Juliet B. Schor & Betsy Taylor*

What if we enacted correctional policies based on these questions: if my son or daughter, father or sister, committed a crime, a terrible crime, what would I want the system to do to them, for them, with them?

— *Christopher Phillips*

Jefferson and Adams read the same Enlightenment texts, but where they amused, consoled, and infuriated Adams, to Jefferson they represented a great magazine of ammunition with which to attack the smug Federalists and all others who emphasized the frailty of men –
the better to exert power over then.

— *Joyce Appleby*

From the cowardice that dare not face new truth,
From the laziness that is contented with half truth,
From the arrogance that thinks it knows all truth,
Good Lord, deliver me.

— *Kenyan prayer*

America was certainly hated all around the world before the Mickey Mouse coup d'état. And we weren't hated, as Bush would have it, because of our liberty and justice for all. We are hated because our corporations have been the principal deliverers and imposers of new technologies and economic schemes that have wrecked cultures.

— *Kurt Vonnegut*

JASON A. MERCHEY

No loss by flood and lightning, no destruction of cities and
temples by the hostile forces of nature has deprived man
of so many noble lives and impulses as those which his
intolerance has destroyed.

— *HELEN KELLER*

Out of the mouths of babes comes truth.

— *OLD TESTAMENT, PSALM 8:1-2*

If we really honor our heroes, why don't we take half of that
big tax cut and give it to the heroes? Or is that why they're
our heroes – because they work cheap?

— *BILL MAHER*

History has a long-range perspective. It ultimately passes stern
judgment on tyrants and vindicates those who fought, suffered,
were imprisoned, and died for human freedom, and against
political oppression and economic slavery.

— *ELIZABETH GURLEY FLYNN*

The law, especially in times of great fear, does not always leave
room for wise decisions.

— *BOB HERBERT*

Misconceptions about love can lead to suffering. For instance,
misconceptions like: "falling in love."

— *M. SCOTT PECK*

The "character myth" relies on the psychological phenomenon
that a person who speaks frequently and passionately about
morals is generally regarded as a moral person. According to
the character myth, a person who demonstrates that he has
"character" need not present any evidence in support of his
policies or decisions. They are simply assumed to be correct,
since they come from a person with the ineffable quality
known as "character."

— *RENANA BROOKS*

FOURTEEN

I have no objection to churches so long as they do not
interfere with God's work.

— *Brooks Atkinson*

The golf [courses] lie so near the mill
That almost every day
The laboring children can look out
And see the men at play.

— *Sarah N. Cleghorn*

This place [prison] is not one in which humanity can survive;
only steel can.

— *Rubin Carter*

The love for justice that is in us is not only the best part of our
being, but it is also the most true to our nature.

— *Cesar Chavez*

    The great thinker Bertrand Russell believed that "Love of truth is the basis of all real virtue...." For example, questions such as, "Does God exist?", "Who let the dogs out?", "Should we use military means to solve this problem?", and "What do I really want out of life?" are timeless questions. They get at whether or not we as a person or as a society are right, are perceiving reality *truly*, and if there is correctness to our belief(s). Issues such as low self-esteem, racism, voluntary warfare, and unquestioning adherence to religious dogma are subject to the sanitizing and clarifying light of truth, should we choose to subject them to it. Socrates' belief that we ought to know ourselves is a reflection of truth: "Know thyself" asks one to "perceive truly what is within you, what makes you 'you,' what you are about." To misperceive aspects of ourselves, the universe, and our relationships seems to account for much human folly throughout history. To know one's self is not easy or pleasant, but it is wise, for as Florida Scott-Maxwell knew: "When you truly possess all that you have been and done...you are fierce with reality."

liberty and, 125, 131, 133, 134
magnanimity and, 149, 154
peace and, 129
truth and, 226

H

happiness
dedication and, 96
fulfillment and, 36, 41, 43, 47, 49
integration and, 179
lightheartedness and, 55, 63
meaning and, 43, 46
modesty and, 18
passion and, 194
responsibility and, 96
self-worth and, 164
will and, 100
hatred
magnanimity and, 151
peace and, 127
health. *see* wellness
history
absurdity and, 55
development and, 174, 185
integration and, 184
justice and, 232, 238
knowledge and, 3, 10
morality and, 110
progressivism and, 186, 188
risk-taking and, 198
truth and, 237
vision and, 84
honesty
humor and, 54
integrity and, 109, 111
morality and, 108, 113
honor. *see also* Honor, Integrity, &
Morality
activism and, 112
character and, 106
death and, 108
development and, 177

gender and, 115
importance of, 109
law and, 121
love and, 107
politics and, 117
respect and, 111
self-worth and, 117
slavery and, 113
truth and, 107
war and, 107, 108, 110, 111, 112, 113,
114, 116
wealth and, 106, 112
Honor, Integrity, & Morality,
105–122
humanism
liberty and, 136
lightheartedness and, 57
magnanimity and, 142
humanity
absurdity and, 56
courage and, 213
development and, 183
ingenuity and, 71
integration and, 180
integrity and, 106, 112
justice and, 227, 232, 239
kindness and, 145, 146
liberty and, 126, 127, 130, 137
magnanimity and, 146, 147, 153
morality and, 111, 113
optimism and, 38, 39
respect and, 20, 28, 29
responsibility and, 93
strength and, 214
tolerance and, 25
truth and, 226, 229, 230, 234
humor. *see also* Humor,
Lightheartedness, & Acceptance
of the Absurd
age and, 55, 57, 58, 63
analysis and, 55
children and, 62, 64, 65, 66
death and, 58

art and, 233
capitalism and, 232
character and, 238
children and, 238
circumspection and, 231, 236
comfort and, 224
consequences and, 226
ecology and, 229
evil and, 234
faith and, 224
fear and, 230
gender and, 230
government and, 226
history and, 237
honor and, 107
humanity and, 226, 229, 230, 234
life and, 234
limitation and, 224, 236
love and, 238
modesty and, 19, 25
morality and, 107, 225
opinion and, 223
patriotism and, 237
politics and, 226, 231
religion and, 227, 232, 235, 239
science and, 227, 235, 237
self-awareness and, 224, 228, 239
self-worth and, 225
society and, 233, 234
strength and, 233, 237
time and, 225
wisdom and, 231, 233
Truth & Justice, 223–240

U

uncertainty
tolerance and, 30
vision and, 82
wisdom and, 8
utility
humor and, 55
wisdom and, 6

V

values. *see also* specific chapters
courage and, 215
dedication and, 99, 145
integrity and, 106
self-worth and, 158
violence
courage and, 212
liberty and, 132
magnanimity and, 155
passion and, 201
peace and, 126, 135, 136
virtues. *see* morality; values
vision. *see also* Creativity,
Ingenuity, & Vision
adversity and, 71, 83
art and, 74, 84
change and, 71
children and, 83
choices and, 73
connection and, 74, 76, 85
development and, 187
discernment and, 75
drugs and, 69
ecology and, 79, 80
education and, 80
entertainment and, 70
experience and, 78, 82, 83
faith and, 70, 74, 75, 76
flexibility and, 76
foresight and, 78
fulfillment and, 74
history and, 84
ideas and, 81
imagination and, 77, 78
introspection and, 70
leadership and, 75, 79
life and, 79
limitation and, 70, 71, 72, 73, 75, 76
patriotism and, 72
philosophy and, 72, 75
possibility and, 73, 83

Ephron, Nora
  on fulfillment, 36
  on humor, 62
Epictetus
  on responsibility, 93
  on self-confidence, 165
Eschenbach, Marie Ebner von
  on self-confidence, 168
  on wisdom, 11
Estefan, Gloria, on development, 174
Exodus 21:23-25, on justice, 226

F

Falk, Richard, on liberty, 133
Farnham, Eliza, on truth, 231
Farrell, Scott
  on altruism, 144
  on courage, 207
  on development, 177
Faulkner, William, on kindness, 146
Feather, William, on integration, 179
Feinstein, Dianne, on strength, 214
Fellini, Federico, on creativity, 80
Ferguson, Marilyn
  on ingenuity, 76
  on respect, 18
  on self-confidence, 163
Fernández, Gigi, on altruism, 145
Fippinger, Faith, on strength, 218
Fisher, Antwone
  on meaning, 43
  on self-worth, 162
  on vision, 73
Fisher, Carrie, on self-confidence, 168
Fiske, Sandra, on self-worth, 169
Fitzgerald, F. Scott, on will, 102
Flynn, Elizabeth Gurley
  on justice, 238
  on morality, 116
Flynn, James R., on vision, 73
Foot, Philippa
  on altruism, 154
  on peace, 138

  on wisdom, 8
Forbes, Malcolm S., on humor, 54
Forbes, Peter, on responsibility, 91
Fox, Matthew,
  on acceptance of the absurd, 66
France, Anatole
  on development, 187
  on passion, 197
Frances, Juana,
  on acceptance of the absurd, 56
Francois, Duc de la Rochefoucauld,
  on strength, 216
Frank, Anne
  on development, 180
  on optimism, 39
  on passion, 195
Franken, Al
  on justice, 228
  on responsibility, 97
Franklin, Benjamin
  on integrity, 109
  on self-confidence, 168
  on truth, 227
  on vision, 79
French, Heather, on dedication, 98
Freud, Anna, on creativity, 79
Freud, Sophie, on truth, 236
Friedan, Betty, on development, 186
Fromm, Erich
  on development, 179
  on integration, 187
  on respect, 32
  on tolerance, 19
  on truth, 230
Frost, Robert
  on passion, 194
  on respect, 27
  on wisdom, 9
Fuemana, Pauly, on peace, 133
Fuentes, Carlos, on respect, 31
Fuller, Buckminster, on strength, 213
Fuller, Margaret, on development, 186
Fuller, Robert W.

values of the wise

Jason Merchey
SPEAKING • SEMINARS • COACHING

Jason is a gifted speaker who has a compelling message for all who wish to deepen their understanding of values, and experience broader and deeper levels of consciousness and greater fulfillment.

He delivers fascinating lectures and stimulating workshops that provide ideas, methods and tools for building a *"life of value."* Jason offers practical approaches to help you define your own values and understand how values motivate and direct your belief systems and the choices you make.

Jason's intellect, insight, creativity and humor make every encounter with him enjoyable and rewarding.

For Jason's conference and seminar schedule and more information on his speaking, seminars, coaching and consulting and VALUES OF THE WISE

Visit **www.valuesofthewise.com**

Or Write To:	VALUES OF THE WISE
	113 West G Street
	Suite 443
	San Diego, California 92101
Call Toll-Free:	866.8.VALUES

VOW
VALUES
of the **WISE**
BRINGING GREAT THINKING TO LIFE℠

287

jason a. merchey

Jason Merchey – philosophical thinker, author, speaker, and coaching consultant was born in Los Angeles and raised in Southern California.

Though an excellent, even precocious, student as a child, family problems affected him deeply and he went into an emotional and intellectual hibernation. It was not until college, when he stumbled across the great thinkers, that he awakened to his life and his purpose. He began to flourish as he discovered his passion for philosophy and wisdom to guide him through difficult times. In Jason's words, "Socrates saved me."

Re-energized, Jason graduated with highest honors in Psychology & Social Behavior, followed by a Master's degree in Psychology. He enjoyed studying the practical aspects of psychology, and was inducted into *Phi Beta Kappa* for liberal scholarship. Jason is proud of the fact that this translates to: Love of Wisdom: The Guide of Life.

During college, Jason attended classes and worked with abused children by day and in restaurants by night. He then moved to San Diego, where he has since been studying and practicing psychotherapy and family therapy. Two issues that interest him are family emotional process and the search for purpose and meaning in life.

Jason has always been intrigued by philosophical and existential thought, and ethics. His affinity for language, combined with strong, progressive, humanistic interests inspired him to research, collect, and catalogue quotations from thousands of notable writers, celebrities, philosophers, and politicians. His favorite quote is by Albert Einstein: *"Understanding the atom is child's play compared to the understanding of the child's play."*

Jason lives and plays with great passion. He is dedicated to inspiring and helping people create "a life of value" by bringing the timeless wisdom of great thinkers to life in books, lectures, and seminars. Jason offers ideas and methods for experiencing broader and deeper levels of thinking, creating greater awareness and fulfillment by discovering one's own values.

www.valuesofthewise.com